The STEWARDSHIP ADVANTAGE

Building a Profitable and Principled Small Business—with the Power to Change the World!

DAVID GRAU SR., JD

THE STEWARDSHIP ADVANTAGE
Building a Profitable and Principled Small Business —with the Power to Change the World!

Book cover design by ebooklaunch.com
Interior layout by Streetlight Graphics

ISBN: 979-8-9998061-0-9

Business Transitions Publishing, LLC
Lexington, KY (US)
Printed in the United States of America

"A single drop of water creates countless ripples."

Anonymous Proverb

OTHER BOOKS BY DAVID GRAU SR., JD:

Acquiring Your Future Through a Succession Plan:

A Primer for Next Gen Professional Service Providers (2025)

Building with the End in Mind:

A Complete Succession Planning Guide for Professional Service Owners (2024)

Buying, Selling, and Valuing Financial Practices (2016)

Succession Planning for Financial Advisors:

Building an Enduring Business (2014)

This book is dedicated to Mary and Robert Powell who make the world a better place every day.

TABLE OF CONTENTS

Introduction 1

Important Notes 4

Part One: THE FOUNDATIONS OF BUSINESS STEWARDSHIP

   1.1 The Business Case for Doing Good 9

   1.2 Discovering and Sharing Your Purpose 15

   1.3 Stewardship and Stakeholders 25

   1.4 The Power of Integrated Stewardship 33

   1.5 The Need for Durability and Long-Term Success 39

   1.6 Myths and Misconceptions 46

   1.7 Considering the B Corporation Model 53

   1.8 The World Needs You Now! 59

   REFERENCES/Part One (in alphabetical order) 64

Part Two: FINDING "THE EXTRA" TO SHARE

   2.1 Setting Up (or Adjusting) a Proper Entity Structure 71

   2.2 Shifting Value to Your Entity 80

   2.3 Understanding How Stock/Equity Is Bought and Sold ... 84

   2.4 Rethinking Your Business's Cash Flows 88

   2.5 Using Profitability as Your Guidepost 95

   2.6 Mastering the Concept of Shareholder Value 105

2.7 Understanding Business Value and Valuation 109

2.8 Generating Strong, Consistent Growth 115

2.9 Building Your Successor Team 121

REFERENCES/Part Two (in alphabetical order) 126

Part Three: CHANGING THE WORLD

3.1 Developing a Stewardship Plan 129

3.2 Integrating Proper Governance Procedures 140

3.3 Crafting Your Legacy through Stewardship 148

3.4 Measuring and Reporting Your Stewardship Impact 155

3.5 The Cold, Hard Business Case 159

3.6 Stakeholder-By-Stakeholder Action Guide 164

REFERENCES/Part Three (in alphabetical order) 177

About the Author 179

Index 181

INTRODUCTION:

I'll be straight with you. I spent more than 30 years working with small business owners—as an attorney, a securities regulator, a consultant, and an author. I helped thousands of entrepreneurs start their businesses, grow them, sell them, and, in many cases, pass them on to key employees or family members through a formal succession plan. From Los Angeles to Boston, and many smaller cities in between, I sat across the table from their lawyers, CPAs, insurance agents, successors, and loved ones. If there was a decision to be made or a plan to be built, I was usually in the room—physically or virtually.

And yet, in all those years and all those meetings, I never once heard anyone talk about small business stewardship. Not one client. Not one advisor. Not one small business owner ever said, "We need to be good stewards of our employees, our community, our supply chain, our environment." I never saw a formal, written stewardship plan. The concept simply didn't seem to exist at the small business level—not in the playbooks I was handed or in the culture I worked in. The closest we came were recycling bins in the break room and occasional charitable donations during the holidays.

When I first began writing this book, I wasn't sure what I would find or learn. I knew stewardship was absent from the business conversations I had participated in for decades. It wasn't showing up in boardrooms, business plans, or hiring and marketing decisions. But I had a growing conviction that there had to be more—that someone, somewhere, had figured out how to practically, and without compromise, run a small business not just for profit, but for people, purpose, and principle. I found plenty of theory about doing good in business, but very little about how to actually implement it in a small business setting. Giving up one conviction for another seemed to be the message—and I didn't like it.

So, as a former attorney, I went looking for the answers and the evidence. And what I found amazed me.

Across industries, countries, and cultures, I discovered small business owners who were quietly, intentionally, and often spectacularly practicing stewardship. They didn't always call it that—but they were doing it. They were building businesses that took care of all their stakeholders and made their communities—and ultimately the world—a better place. They prioritized doing right over doing easy, and for the most part, no one even noticed. I found dozens of these companies through virtual research, but I know there are hundreds, if not thousands, out there—in a world where we need tens of millions.

In a way, this book is one long origin story—not just mine, but the stories of dozens of small business owners and leaders from around the world who are already showing us what stewardship looks like in action. You'll meet them in the Stewardship Spotlights throughout this book. They are proof that stewardship is not only possible—it's already happening. Quietly. Globally. Powerfully. And now, maybe, through you.

If you choose, you can build something that lasts and makes a real difference. You can lead with purpose and earn a strong profit in a principled business. You can take better care of your employees, customers, community, suppliers, partners, and the planet—and in doing so, create a business that matters more than you may realize, and a world you can be proud to hand off to your children and grandchildren. In Part Two, I'll help you find the extra to work with, to share, as you build a stronger, better business. In Part Three, I'll show you how to document these processes, track your success, and make it work—one step, one stakeholder at a time.

That's what this book is about. *The Stewardship Advantage* is a bold new strategy for small business owners who want to grow strong profits and an even stronger legacy—by leading with principle, purpose, and a commitment to real-world impact. This is a way to operationalize *doing good*. And as you'll read later in Part One, the world really needs you now.

But let me pause to acknowledge something important. Not every business owner wakes up wanting to change the world—and that's okay. Stewardship doesn't require a cape or a global mission. It begins with showing up for your people, doing right by your customers, paying attention to your vendors, and leaving things better than you found them. Taking care of your own stakeholders—systematically, methodically, and purposefully—is like dropping a pebble into a still pond. You may not see the full reach of that ripple, but it's there, traveling farther than you think. And when those quiet, small ripples multiply—business by business, leader by leader—they can become a wave powerful enough to create lasting, meaningful change. That's what small business stewardship is.

And now, you're the one holding the pebble.

So turn the page, and let me show you how to build a small business that lasts. A small business that matters. One that leaves behind more than a balance sheet— even while you make a great living. This is modern business building, with real and lasting impact in mind.

That's what makes this book different.

IMPORTANT NOTES:

1. **This book is written for small business owners everywhere.** I believe small businesses and their owners hold the key to solving many of the world's greatest challenges based on the simple notion that doing good, is good business. Taking care of ALL of your stakeholders is the path to greatest personal and financial success. To become a better leader who can build a stronger and enduring business, you have to help all of your stakeholders become better as well; what helps them helps you. This simple but powerful approach transcends borders. It connects a practical strategy to build a profitable and principled business with the greater power to change the world.

2. **I am a champion of shared ownership.** Two owners are better than one. Three owners are better than two. Equity in a small business should be earned, not given away; it is the risk that gives meaning to the investment. Owners who invest where they work tend to invest where they live. I believe in multi-owner firms as a path to long-term strength, shared leadership, and community stewardship. We'll explore this further in Part Two. This is the key to building a small business that lasts and continues to make a difference on behalf of all of its stakeholders for generations to come.

3. **This is not a political or religious book.** Stewardship, in its truest sense, is the careful and responsible management of something entrusted to one's care. It is not directly tied to any ideology, party, or belief system. It is simply part of being human and, in this case, being an owner and leader of a small business. That said, wherever you find your motivation, purpose and principle to be a good steward, hold onto it—and let it guide you.

4. **Throughout this book, you'll find Stewardship Spotlights.** These short profiles highlight real businesses making a meaningful difference through

intentional stewardship of their people, resources, and communities. None were paid mentions. I selected them based on their efforts and stories. I did limited due diligence from a distance—reading websites, customer reviews, impact statements, and public reports—but I'm not going to equivocate here. These stewards deserve your support. Go meet them. Thank them. Order from them. You can learn more at www.DavidGrauSr.com and even nominate other small business stewards that you know. These are the real heroes of this story.

5. **A note about "Fortune 500+" references.** Technically, Fortune 500 companies are the 500 largest U.S. firms by revenue, as ranked by *Fortune* magazine. When I use the term "Fortune 500+/company+" in this book, I'm referring more broadly to the largest companies in your region—Fortune Europe 500, Fortune China 500, Global 500, and so on. This book is written for a global audience of small business leaders.

6. **All key facts, figures, and quotes** within the text of this book are referenced at the end of Part One, Part Two, and Part Three, in alphabetical order. Every effort has been taken to provide accurate, verifiable citations and to properly credit the sources of information used in this book.

7. **Many initiatives, one calling.** There are countless organizations, ideas, and acronyms dedicated to making the world a better place, especially in the areas of sustainability, ethics, and corporate responsibility. A few of the better-known include:

- 1% for the Planet
- B Corporations
- Benevity
- CDP (Carbon Disclosure Project)
- CSR (Corporate Social Responsibility)
- Conscious Capitalism
- DEI (Diversity, Equity, and Inclusion)
- ESG (Environmental, Social, and Governance)
- Earth911
- FTF (Fair Trade Federation)

- Fair Trade Certification
- Fair for Life
- GBCI (Green Business Certification, Inc.)
- GRI (Global Reporting Initiative)
- SDGs (Sustainable Development Goals)
- SEWF (Social Enterprise World Forum)
- SRI (Sustainable and Responsible Investing)
- Steward-Ownership
- Supplier Partnership Ethics
- TBL (Triple Bottom Line)
- The B Team

Every one of these, and many others, was founded with the best of intentions. Each represents a different approach to doing better whether focused on the environment, transparency, trade, social equity, or governance and their leadership should be commended. And yet, each has its staunch critics. That's the world we live in: abundant with alternatives, yet fragmented in focus. Too many frameworks. Too few participants under each banner. Too much energy spent building parallel systems rather than uniting around common ground.

To truly make a difference in the world, we don't need a hundred initiatives pulling in different directions. We need tens of millions of small businesses working together under one shared banner. What if that banner was called **stewardship**?

What if small, principled business owners around the globe picked up the stewardship mantle and made it their own advantage? What if we stopped waiting for top-down solutions and instead built from the ground up—one owner, one business, one community at a time? Small businesses already have the numbers. Their owners have the drive. They live where they work. They show up early, stay late, and roll up their sleeves on Saturday mornings while others sleep in. They know their people. They care. And that's why stewardship belongs to them, and to you.

As your guide—and as a small business owner who has done much of what I now ask you to consider—I offer a practical truth: You don't need a certification to care. You don't need a global program to give. You don't need permission to do what's right. All you need is a sense of responsibility and the willingness to act on it. Change starts with a small group of motivated people who share a vision, work together, and do more than just earn a living. Respectfully so.

Now imagine the impact of a million such businesses in one country. Or fifty million around the world. That should give us all hope. Let's figure this out, together.

PART ONE:
THE FOUNDATIONS OF BUSINESS STEWARDSHIP

1.1 THE BUSINESS CASE FOR DOING GOOD

I'm glad you are reading this book, but I will not take your interest and your time for granted. Small business owners always have more work to do. I have a message of importance and business-changing, maybe even life-changing advice to deliver, but the work and the effort will fall on you. Still, I am at least partly responsible for answering the seminal question: Why should you care about using your small business to help those around you—all of your stakeholders (a term specifically defined in Section 1.3)? Why should you build a principled business and consistently share your extra time, money, energy and talents to help others on your staff, in your community, your supply chain, or even people on the other side of the world?

The honest answers are layered, and demanding:

- Because you can. You had the courage and grit to start something from nothing. You chose to build, to lead, to take the harder but more meaningful road. That takes principle: a decision to act with integrity even when no one is watching.

- Because you are needed. You have the ability—and increasingly, the responsibility—to do what others cannot. With your business and your team, you are not just creating value; you are multiplying it. You can build something that outlasts your career, something worthy of being passed down.

- Because doing good is good business. When you invest in those around you, they invest back—in your success, your vision, and your growth. But more than that, principled actions earn trust. And trust is the most valuable business currency there is.

- Because relying solely on government and taxation to solve social problems has never been enough. As a small business owner, you are close to the ground. You know your people. You know your community. You are perfectly positioned to respond with compassion, speed, and care. Principle gives that power its purpose.

- Because the world is struggling—and it needs your help, now. It needs your energy, your kindness, your fairness, your creativity, and your resolve.

Every day, small business owners make decisions that impact their employees, customers, suppliers, and communities. It is personal, and that makes it powerful. And there are hundreds of millions of small businesses nestled away in small communities and situated on the corners of the busiest avenues in the largest cities of the world. Small businesses and their leaders are everywhere, and they touch everyone. And when it's guided by principle and purpose, it becomes a force for real and lasting change.

Before I retired as a small business owner, I found that I liked things that I had control over. Being a business owner gave me that ability, and I don't just mean in an organizational sense. The specifics of those past operational decisions aren't the things I now remember decades later. What I do remember is that we could pay small, surprise bonuses to special employees because they deserved it, or buy movie tickets for everyone that came in to work on the last Friday of a hard month. We could cater lunch on Fridays for the entire crew. We could pay the annual premiums for a key employee's whole life insurance policy to provide him/her some peace of mind, or anonymously buy dinner for a table full of returning veterans at an airport restaurant on our way through. We could give a special person a weekend at the coast, a gift certificate to a local spa, or sponsor a local Little League or softball team. As a group, we could volunteer to cook dinner for two dozen people at a local

Ronald McDonald House. I could quietly and quickly put a hundred-dollar bill in the tip jar of my favorite coffee place every holiday season just to make their day really special and make them wonder who they had pleased and what they had done to deserve such a reward.

Most of these examples are good deeds and you have likely done much the same, but stewardship, and benefiting from the stewardship advantage as you will learn, is very different. In this book, you'll learn how to integrate stewardship into the DNA of your business; to operationalize it. But before we unpack the full definition, responsibilities, and capabilities of stewardship, let me offer a few more pointed reasons why sharing your resources and caring for your stakeholders is not just generous and kind–it is smart, fulfilling, and good business:

a) **Being a good steward will make your small business stronger and more valuable.** That is not just the premise of this book, it is the foundation of a sustainable business. Stewardship is not a cost or an obligation. It is an investment that multiplies.

b) **Stewardship starts where you are.** As a small business owner and good steward, you live and work in the same communities as your customers, employees, and suppliers. The environment starts right outside your front door. You see the needs and feel the benefits firsthand. And because you have *feet on the ground*, you are in the best position to respond with real solutions—not bureaucracy, not distant programs, but real action. It is your community. It is your responsibility. It is your opportunity.

c) **Compassion plays a critical role in effective small business leadership.** You cannot be a good steward without genuinely caring. A compassionate owner leads with their head, guided by their heart, recognizing that a thriving business is built on trust, fairness, and a deep empathy that ultimately drives action. Caring is not soft or weak. It is smart. It is forward thinking. It is human. It is how relationships, and businesses, grow stronger over time.

d) **People want to be part of something bigger than themselves.** Employees don't come to work to make the owner rich. They come to do meaningful work, contribute to something they believe in too, and grow as people (in addition to the paycheck!). Offering someone a job is good. Offering them a purpose is better. Do that for a generation, and you change lives. That is what great leadership looks like. We will build on this in the pages that follow.

e) **Treat your stakeholders well and you'll benefit in ways you never expected.** I believe kindness is rewarded. It's either returned directly or passed along to others. In the seventies, we called it karma. Today, we just know it's true: actions have consequences. And the good ones often echo louder and longer than we realize. Even decades later, past stewardship still brings me comfort and pride.

f) **The shift in customer expectations is creating a tailwind for small business stewardship.** In recent years, a powerful shift has taken root in customer behavior. More people are actively seeking alternatives to large, impersonal corporations. They want transparency, connection, values, and a sense that their money is going toward something meaningful. They're tired of scripted call centers and policies written by legal departments. Instead, they're drawn to businesses that know their name, stand for something, and treat every transaction as a relationship—not a line item.

Stewardship is where small businesses have a unique and growing advantage. Stewardship is no longer just the *right* way to run a business, it is also what an increasing number of customers *want*. A small business that treats its employees well, sources responsibly, supports its community, and communicates with sincerity doesn't just stand apart—it stands ahead. For owners willing to lean into this moment, the opportunity is not just to survive against bigger players, but to thrive *because* you're different.

g) **At a certain point in life, we all ask: What does it all mean? Why does it matter?** Using your small business to serve something beyond personal profit can provide a deep sense of purpose—not just now, but especially in hindsight. When you look back, it won't be your margins that you remember (even though we will not compromise on profitability in the small business stewardship process). It will be the people you helped, the lives you touched, and the difference you made. That, too, is a legacy.

The stewardship advantage is a strategy for small business owners who believe that by taking better care of their employees, customers, and communities, they can build stronger, more profitable companies—and a better world at the same time.

Small business stewardship requires focus, consistency, and duration. Smartly strengthening your small business will allow for consistent and purposeful support of your goals over the long term. Building a stronger business will, in turn, generate the extra resources needed to support your ongoing stewardship efforts. I often read about businesses needing to learn how to do more with less in order to help others. I do not agree; I don't think that is a long-term solution to anything. The message in this book is the exact opposite. I want to help you do more *with more*! Stewardship is not an obligation, it is not a hinderance, it is an opportunity.

Like any business skill, stewardship is something that must be learned and practiced. Ultimately, the decision of whether and how to use your small business to make the world a better place is a personal one. In the last section of this book, I will list many different ways that you can use your small business to make a real and lasting difference, though not at the expense of making a good living. Balancing the power to run a great business and do good is up to you. But just imagine the satisfaction of being able to improve the lives of everyone you come into contact with as a business owner! And imagine the impact of tens of millions of your peers doing the same.

In return for your consideration, I will share with you some practical yet powerful techniques for running a more profitable, valuable, and investable small business that might just outlive you and certainly your career. The goal is to help you become stronger and richer and better through good stewardship. That is what I have spent my career doing. The cumulative effect of these efforts creates a powerful ripple effect, demonstrating that even the smallest business can be a potent agent of change.

STEWARDSHIP SPOTLIGHT

KING ARTHUR BAKING COMPANY (NORWICH, VERMONT): The King Arthur Baking Company, formerly known as the King Arthur Flour Company, is an American supplier of flour, baking mixes, cookbooks, and baked goods. Founded in Boston, Massachusetts, in 1790, it holds the distinction of being the oldest flour company in the United States.

In 1996, King Arthur transitioned to a 100 percent employee-owned small business structure through an employee stock ownership plan (ESOP), with approximately 100 employees at the time. The move to employee ownership was a natural extension of the company's existing values, reinforcing its commitment to shared success. Since then, King Arthur Baking Company has grown significantly and now employs several hundred people. The ESOP was a catalyst for that growth, not merely a result of it.

King Arthur Baking Company is also a Certified B Corporation, underscoring its dedication to social and environmental responsibility alongside its employee-ownership structure.

1.2 DISCOVERING AND SHARING YOUR PURPOSE

"*WHY* ARE YOU HERE?"

I blinked hard at the questioner seated behind his three-hundred-pound Steelcase desk. I was barely in my twenties. My mouth went dry. I wished for a drink of water. I said something along the lines of, "Beg your pardon?" I had heard my dad say that, and it always seemed like a good way to buy some time to think and find the right words, or any words.

My potential future boss stood up, walked around his desk and stepped towards me, and as we stood face-to-face, he repeated the question more demandingly. "*Why* … are …you …here?"

I had just walked into his office. First time I ever met the guy. In the back of my mind, I wondered if I'd walked into the wrong office. I silently wished I had. I briefly thought about retreating behind the lone chair on my side of the desk, but I could not move. Silence filled the air. No one said anything for what seemed like a full minute. I could literally hear the seconds tick off on the big, old, dusty, industrial clock on the wall. It felt as if I was alone in the center of a stadium filled with tens of thousands of spectators, and every eye in the house was staring intently, expectantly, at me... waiting for the answer. Mentally, I was madly searching for one. Why *was* I here?

I had prepared meticulously for this interview. I really needed the job. My tie had been carefully picked out and knotted quite neatly, I thought. My white, oxford, button-down shirt was spotless. I felt totally out of my league. Home computers weren't a thing yet, at least not in my house, and I'd never heard of Steve Jobs, so I had prepared for the interview at the local public library. I had even visited the local

Hallmark® bookstore to ensure I had the most current information. I had read all I could to prepare for my first important job interview. However, I didn't remember ever reading this particular question.

Forty-five years or so later, my memory isn't clear as to how I answered the question or what I said, but I got the job. I knew not to say anything like "I need the money," but I am not sure if I did much better. In the subsequent years, and after many years of college and study, I often thought back to that moment in time. I wondered, had I been brave enough and smart enough, what would have happened if I had answered my half of the Q&A and then turned it around and asked him, "Sir, why is *this company* here? What is its purpose in the world? In my life?" Sure wish I would have known enough to ask those questions! It might have cost me the interview, but I would have loved to hear the answers.

The point is that purpose matters, and we all need to find our own answers. Stewardship doesn't create purpose, it follows it. When you know what you stand for, stewardship becomes the way you live it out. To everyone associated with a small business—its owners and employees and their significant others, its suppliers, customers, future owners/investors, even supporting accountants, attorneys, and financial advisors—purpose matters, and it matters even more if you build *on purpose*. That is a choice you have. So, I will put the same question to you: "Why are *you* here?"

My goal is to help you figure out the answer in the first one-third of this book, or Part One. As a professional traveler, I can attest that it is always best to know where you are going before you get there. This is the first step on the pathway to making a difference in the world.

I've started three small businesses in my life. Two of those businesses I thought would become much larger and valuable than anyone could imagine. They didn't. The other business I thought would do okay and might just make me a decent living. It far exceeded my expectations and continues on after my retirement. You never know, so you work equally hard on each, and give it your all. But I did not start any of these businesses specifically aiming for high profitability, tax efficiency, or lots of partners. I did not build with a specific stewardship goal in mind, like the environment or my staff's well-being. I wasn't looking for people and worthy causes to share my imaginary future fortune with. Maybe I should have. Mostly, I just wanted to share my ideas, my enthusiasm, and my knowledge with a grateful clientele; do something on my own; *and make a good living*–the goals of many a small business owner. There are bills to pay, work to do, and dreams to achieve.

So where do you start as a small business owner? I am going to lay it out here on the first pages of Part One because you must be able to articulate your purpose, and separately, your vision and your goals first and foremost. What do you stand for? Even small organizations can foster purpose by connecting work to a greater mission. But if you are not clear about these issues as a leader and an owner, it is hard for anyone to follow and support you.

To make a difference as an organized group (even of just two or three people), you have to stand for something or be about something that those you encounter understand and can get behind. The best place to start, coming from an English major, is to write it down. It is called a **mission statement,** and few small business owners get this part right, if they even take the time to try. A mission statement is the foundational purpose of a business. It outlines what the business aims to achieve and often reflects its core values. A carefully crafted statement can act as a compass for your decision-making, helping you to filter opportunities and stay focused on what truly matters, saving you time and resources in the long run.

Your mission statement clearly communicates your business's identity to customers, current and potential employees and partners, and serves as a powerful motivator for your team, especially during challenging times. The guidelines are simple and brief. Your mission statement should set forth the general values and principles which guide your work as an organization, and answer the following questions:

- Who are we?

- What do we do?

- Why do we do it?

- For whom do we do it?

Keep in mind that this is not a backwards looking exercise. The point of this process is to know where you are going! The key elements of an effective mission statement are these:

- Clarity (it should be easy to understand);

- Focus (it should highlight your core services and target audience);

- Value (it should emphasize the benefits you provide to your clients);

- Conciseness (it should be short and to the point).

It is your mission statement, and you can write what you like and adjust it over time. Defining your purpose, even in a book about stewardship, is not about altruism—you have a business to run! Let's consider some well-known examples of mission statements that have served other businesses well. This exercise will help you understand how simple and straightforward such statements can be, even for much larger business models (when it comes to learning new things, I will not discriminate against big business). Think of this exercise as peering over the fence at a large construction site to see and learn what is going on inside.

"Responsibility is not a burden, it is a blessing."

John Ralston Saul
(Canada)

McDonalds™ Corporation's mission statement is "To make delicious feel-good moments easy for everyone." McDonald's mission and values have certainly evolved over time. The company's original focus, when founded by the McDonald brothers in 1940 and later expanded by Ray Kroc, was on *fast service, quality food, and cleanliness*. These principles are still reflected in their current values, but the mission statement has broadened to encompass the "feel-good moments" aspect, a key part of the company's evolution.

The Coca-Cola™ Company's mission statement is "To refresh the world and make a difference." This concise and powerful statement encapsulates the company's core purpose. It highlights not only the physical refreshment that their beverages seek to provide, but also the broader impact they aim to have on the world, encompassing or implying social, environmental, and economic aspects. These are two examples of mission statements that help to guide just over $73 billion in combined gross revenue last year, and over $19 billion in net profits. Impressive, but obviously these are not small businesses. So, let's bring this down to earth.

The Bombas™ company (Bombas, LLC), a comfort focused sock and apparel brand with a mission to help those in need, is still privately owned and has around 200 employees. Their core mission from day one has been to help those experiencing homelessness based on a "one-purchased, one-donated" social initiative. To date, based on Bombas's own impact reports, this company has donated over 100 million clothing items to more than 3,500 community organizations for distribution. This is a great and rare example of a small business that has made it their purpose from day one to change the world for the better while still generating a profit for their investors. Their entire business model and website is effectively their mission statement and purpose for being.

Many businesses are much smaller than Bombas. You do not need 200 employees, or even twenty, to make a difference and change the world. Here are some examples of other great small-company mission statements:

- To empower creators to make their best work and get it in front of the audience they deserve.

- To provide exceptional customer service and a unique range of products.

- To build healthier communities by connecting people to real food.

- To inspire and impact the world with vision, purpose, and style.

- To create and promote great-tasting, healthy, organic beverages.

- To make it easy to do business anywhere.

Let's get more specific. Here are mission statements for a variety of small business models:

For a small consulting firm: "Our mission is to empower small and mid-sized businesses with practical, strategic guidance—helping them grow sustainably, operate more effectively, and make a meaningful impact in their industries and communities."

For an accounting firm: "Our mission is to provide accurate, timely, and trustworthy accounting services that help small business owners make informed financial decisions, stay compliant, and build stronger, more resilient companies, so they can focus on what matters most."

For a boutique marketing agency: "We craft brand stories with purpose and precision—delivering creative, data-driven marketing strategies that drive measurable results and meaningful connections."

For a financial planning business: "Our mission is to provide personalized, values-aligned financial guidance, empowering clients to build secure, confident futures for themselves and their families."

For a small IT support company: "Our mission is to deliver reliable and efficient IT solutions, enabling our clients to focus on their core business operations without technology disruptions."

For a small legal firm: "To provide dedicated and ethical legal counsel, ensuring our clients receive personalized representation and achieve favorable outcomes."

For an independent bookstore: "To cultivate a love of reading by providing curated book selections and a welcoming space for literary exploration."

Though the final decision and preference belongs to every small business owner or ownership team, a mission statement should be between one to three sentences in length, generally not to exceed 100 words. Together, your mission statement and your small business can support a world where people work to make a good life, not just a good living.

Once you have begun to figure out your mission statement, share it with others and keep thinking about it. Having a written or stated purpose is not the goal—it is a starting place. Doing something with that purpose, turning your ideals into actions in your community and becoming a force for good, is what matters. Just as profits support a business and its investors, purpose and meaning support the people and employees that work at that business every day and the customers the business attracts and serves. Tell them, simply, what you are all about.

Let's expand this exploration and thinking. Many businesses quickly evolve this process into a *mission, vision, purpose statement*. Your **mission** is what you actually *do* right now—who you serve and how you operate day-to-day to achieve your purpose and work towards your vision. Your **vision** is the big picture of where you are heading—what does success look like for your business? Your **purpose** is the core reason your business exists beyond just making money. It is the underlying need you fill or the problem you solve for people.

Revisiting one of our previous examples, McDonald's Corporation has separate mission, vision, and purpose statements:

- **Mission Statement:** "To make delicious feel-good moments easy for everyone."

- **Vision Statement:** "To move with velocity to drive profitable growth and become an even better McDonald's serving more customers delicious food each day around the world."

- **Purpose Statement:** "To feed and foster communities."

These three, separate statements are interconnected and work together to define and communicate the company's goals and values. Sometimes, simpler is better, or at least a bit easier. To that end, here are some examples of how small businesses *blended* their mission/vision/purpose statements to include elements of good stewardship of their stakeholders (terms that will be specifically defined in the next section):

For an independent coffee shop: "To craft exceptional coffee and create a welcoming gathering place where neighbors connect, while stewarding relationships with farmers, sourcing responsibly, and supporting local artisans and community well-being."

For a local bakery: "To nourish our community with wholesome, handcrafted baked goods—while practicing responsible resource stewardship, supporting our team with care, and contributing to a thriving, connected neighborhood."

For an accounting firm: "We deliver reliable, transparent accounting solutions that empower small business owners to make confident decisions, strengthen their operations, and be good stewards of their financial resources, for the benefit of their teams, customers, and communities."

For a small-scale furniture maker: "To steward the craft of furniture-making by creating heirloom-quality pieces using sustainable materials and time-honored techniques that offer lasting value, beauty, and purpose for generations to come."

For a tech consulting firm: "To serve as trusted stewards of innovation, delivering thoughtful, reliable technology solutions that help our clients thrive, while fostering a culture of integrity, collaboration, and shared growth within our team."

For a family-owned hardware store: "To serve our community with trusted products, honest advice, and meaningful service, stewarding lasting relationships and a resilient, family-run business that stands the test of time."

For an organic farm: "To steward the land and nourish our community by growing healthy, delicious food through regenerative practices, caring for people, soil, and future generations."

As you can see, these statements do not need to be complicated, and you do not need to hire anyone to do this for you. Write it down, share it, and adjust it over time until it communicates what you want to say to the world and to your team. Adjust your statement occasionally as your business grows or as the world changes.

When crafting your own mission, vision, and purpose statement(s), consider which aspects of stewardship are most important to your business and your values. Be specific and authentic in your language to create a statement that truly reflects your commitment to responsible ownership. True stewardship comes from understanding your purpose, not just copying or simulating others' successful actions.

"The best way to find yourself is to lose yourself in the service of others."

Mahatma Gandhi
(India)

You may also have noticed that not one of these statements focused on profits, per se, treating that element more as a result of a well-run business rather than as a primary goal. We will delve more into this important issue in the pages to come, but let's anchor our journey to the underlying themes in this book.

The first is this: FOCUS + CONSISTENCY + DURATION = GOOD STEWARDSHIP

Each of these elements will be expanded on throughout this book. This deceptively simple formula separates stewardship from good intentions and good deeds and is how the strength of many small businesses can change the world. Being a good steward is a continuous, proactive commitment to responsibly managing your small business—its resources, people, and impact—to ensure its long-term health and to benefit all its stakeholders. Good deeds are moments in time; stewardship is a mindset. To succeed in your role as a good steward of your small business, you need a clear purpose, a good plan, and a profitable business.

Second, in the course of my research and writing, I came across many white papers and articles, and a few books, written about how and why purpose should transcend profits. Another common criticism of businesses in general was phrased as "profits before people" or "profit first businesses." Those are interesting arguments or concerns, but they do not reflect the practical reality of running a small business. As a former small business owner, I don't see the possibility of positioning profitability as a choice or as a lower priority. The problem is that most of these arguments have no context. Are we talking about profitability levels at a Fortune 500 company+? A sole proprietorship or a small business with fifteen combined owners and employees? In Section 1.4 below, you can look at the failure rates of small businesses for yourself. At the small business level, as we use and define the term in this book, people and profits are not mutually exclusive; they are mutually reinforcing.

Finally, we will also talk about finding or building "the extra" time, money, and talent to share with your community as you use your small business to change the world. My assumption is that, as a small business, you have limited resources and there is only so much to go around, at least in the early years. What you currently earn, and then some, is already committed. But what if you learn how to build a stronger, more profitable, more valuable, and more investable business and you have more resources to share for a longer period? Well, that would change everything, wouldn't it?

STEWARDSHIP SPOTLIGHT

ECOALF (MADRID, SPAIN): ECOALF is a global leader in developing and utilizing recycled materials—including plastic bottles recovered from the ocean, discarded fishing nets, recycled cotton, and recycled nylon—to create sustainable fashion products. Founded in 2009, ECOALF's mission is to halt the careless use of natural resources by producing recycled products that match the quality, design, and durability of the best conventional products on the market.

The company has developed over 400 different recycled fabrics and uses GRS-certified materials to ensure that its sourcing meets strict environmental and ethical standards. ECOALF is committed to becoming a NET ZERO brand by 2030.

The name ECOALF combines "eco," representing ecology and environmental responsibility, with "Alf," for Alfredo, the founder Javier Goyeneche's eldest son—symbolizing a personal connection to future generations and the company's deep commitment to protecting the planet. In 2021, ECOALF was recognized as a "Best for the World" B Corporation for its environmental leadership.

1.3 STEWARDSHIP AND STAKEHOLDERS

So what exactly is stewardship in the context of a small business? Academically, stewardship is defined as the act of taking care of something on behalf of someone else. In decades past, stewardship in a business setting was all about maximizing value for the shareholders. Today, many business owners equate stewardship with sustainability, or taking care of our planet and its limited resources. The environment is certainly an important stakeholder, but it is just one part of the story. Small business stewardship, as the term is used throughout this book, is a strategy of ownership grounded in responsibility—where value is created for *all* stakeholders, not just or primarily for the shareholders.

The easiest way to understand the role of stewardship in a small business setting is to make a list of your stakeholders and then divide that list into two groups: the internal stakeholders (your current and future team, and the underlying business/ entity structure), and the external stakeholders (clients, suppliers, your community, and the environment). Depending on the size of your business, its location, and its purpose, you might add to or change this list slightly, but these are the common stakeholders (or *stakeholder groups* as most categories represent more than a single person, company, or cause) for a small business:

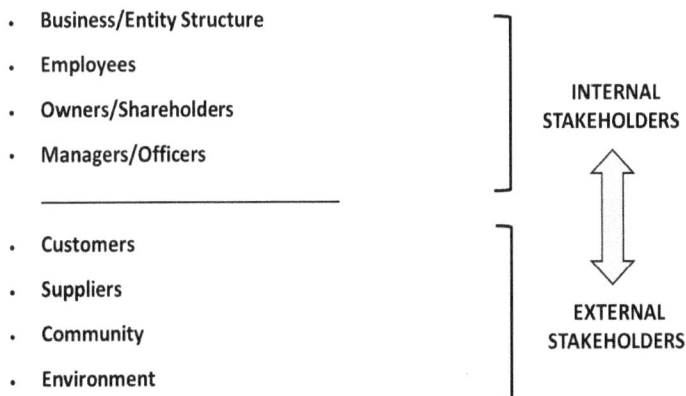

- Business/Entity Structure
- Employees
- Owners/Shareholders
- Managers/Officers

INTERNAL STAKEHOLDERS

- Customers
- Suppliers
- Community
- Environment

EXTERNAL STAKEHOLDERS

Figure 1

Most small businesses don't start out on day one with a plan to be good stewards to all of their stakeholders; that comes later. An owner's first task is to build a viable business. To become a better leader who can build a stronger business, you have to help all of your internal stakeholders become better as well; what helps them helps you.

Building a business that can change the world, one community at a time, necessarily starts with the people who directly support that business and make it successful, and then expands outward to the people in that business's community, to the environment, and to the world. A small business, of course, could be just one or two people—the owner and an employee, or one or two owners. A small business could also be thirty to forty people, or many more. It matters where you start your journey, but it matters more that you lay out and follow a good path. Being a good, consistent steward is much more than a desire to help or make a difference; it is about building a foundation to support the business and its stewardship efforts for many years.

To that end, and before proceeding further, I should explain the inclusion of a business entity structure as a stakeholder. A stakeholder can be defined as any individual, group, organization, company, or entity that has a vested interest in the success and sustainability of the business at issue, and whose well-being is intertwined with the business' operations and decisions. The choice of entity structure directly dictates the legal liability of the business owners, as well as tax implications. This legal structure establishes the rules for ownership, management, and decision-making within a business. This framework dictates how the business can operate, raise capital, and plan for the future. A well-chosen structure can enhance efficiency and attract investment, benefiting all other stakeholders. Fifty years from now, the entity structure may well be the only surviving aspect of the original small business; theoretically, it is immortal.

Within this business/entity framework, a valuable, growing small businesses will find it advantageous to delegate authority to non-owners. The term "Managers," as applied to a stakeholder/stakeholder group, can be used synonymously with a team leader or a supervisor. It does not necessarily mean a Manager-managed Limited Liability Company in which the Managers often function as Directors of the business. To this end, many small businesses will not install a Board of Directors until they grow past about twenty-five to thirty total owners/employees. Officers refers to the traditional roles of Chief Executive Officer, Chief Operating Officer, Chief Financial Officer, and so on; these individuals commonly are owners but are not required to be.

A two-tiered system: Being a good steward and building a strong business requires supporting all of your internal stakeholders. Your internal stakeholders comprise *your bench*, or the talent base that will help your business become more valuable, profitable, investable, and durable. Think of this group as **Tier One**.

This same group is charged with carrying out the business's mission, vision, and value statement(s), and looking after the external stakeholders on a consistent and long-term basis. Your key employees, perhaps including one or more of your family members, may work for the business and may, or may not, become future equity partners. These same key employees may be managers, supervisors, team leaders, or officers. For all these reasons and more, laying a strong foundation for and through the internal stakeholders is the first step in the stewardship process.

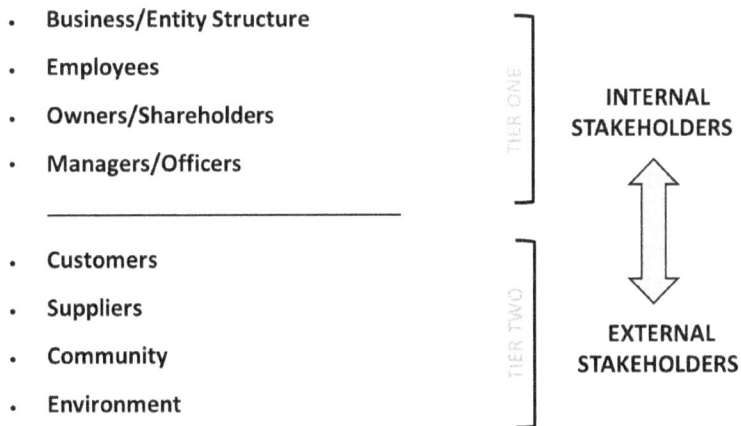

- Business/Entity Structure
- Employees
- Owners/Shareholders
- Managers/Officers

_____

- Customers
- Suppliers
- Community
- Environment

TIER ONE

TIER TWO

INTERNAL
STAKEHOLDERS

EXTERNAL
STAKEHOLDERS

Figure 2

For most small businesses, the **external stakeholders, or Tier Two,** center on the clients or customers without whom there is no business. The favored suppliers, at least in the early years of a small business, are often the most reliable, most affordable, and most immediate options available. Policing one's supply chain takes time and, without a clear mission, vision, purpose statement to guide *you*, it is hard to guide such a stakeholder. The community—whether that is your small town or the city you live in or near, or something larger or different based on your mission, vision, and purpose for being; and/or the environment in general—are often an afterthought at the beginning. Until your small business is stable and you build enough extra to share, the stakeholders are those that are absolutely essential to your operations and success. We should assume that a small business will naturally prioritize its clients or customers. This two-tier, interdependent system of stewardship is how we will navigate this important terrain throughout this book.

Here is an analogy for stewardship of a small business using this two-tiered system. The setting is a family home and its role in the neighborhood and greater community.

TIER ONE (Internal Stakeholders). Before you can serve the world well, you must first take care of your own house:

- Owners are like the parents or guardians of the home. They're responsible for its long-term well-being—ensuring financial stability, maintaining the space, and planning for the future. They are responsible for keeping the home structurally sound for today's needs and tomorrow's generations.

- Managers/Officers are like the household coordinators—those who manage the daily logistics, schedules, and responsibilities. They help translate the owners' long-term vision into daily action, ensuring that the home runs smoothly, decisions are made thoughtfully, and everyone's contributions are aligned.

- Employees are like the members of the household. They contribute to daily life—the energy, upkeep, and culture of the home. A good steward ensures every household member feels safe, supported, and equipped to contribute meaningfully to the home's success.

- The Business/Entity is the structure itself—the foundation, walls, roof, plumbing, and systems. If this framework is weak or neglected, everything else inside is at risk. It's the legal and operational structure that holds everything together and allows it all to function.

TIER TWO (External Stakeholders). Once your house (the business) is in good order, you can turn your attention outward—being a good neighbor in a shared world:

- **Customers** are like visitors or guests who come to your home. They rely on you for comfort, consistency, and a positive experience. A good host anticipates their needs, exceeds expectations, and welcomes them with care and respect.

- **Suppliers** are like the service providers who help keep your household running—grocers, utility workers, plumbers, delivery drivers. Reliable relationships with these partners are essential for a smooth and resilient household. The same goes for your business.

- **Community** is your broader neighborhood—the people, organizations, and culture that surround your home. Good stewardship means contributing to that community's health—supporting events, helping neighbors, and being present in ways that strengthen collective well-being. The community as a stakeholder may represent hundreds—or even thousands—of individual lives.

- **The Environment** is the shared air, water, land, and resources that affect all homes. A good steward is mindful of environmental impact—not just to protect their own home, but to safeguard the health of the entire neighborhood, city, and ultimately the planet. This is the broadest circle of responsibility, and it touches all 8.1 billion of us, "because there is no Planet B" as the good folks at ECOALF, in Madrid, wisely tell us.

Part Two of this book is entirely dedicated to providing ideas and direction to reset the table as to your internal stakeholders. Specific ideas to support these internal and external stakeholders, or stakeholder groups, are listed in Part Three of this book.

The point is, and to complete the analogy, before you can be a good neighbor and a contributing member of the community, you need to get your own house in order. You need to ensure the foundation and walls are solid, the roof isn't leaking, all the bills are paid, and everyone within the household is functioning and interacting well. If your own house is chaotic or falling apart, or your team members are not dependable or aligned with your goals, you won't be in a good position to help or engage well in the wider neighborhood.

Learning to be a good steward highlights that taking care of the business is not just a self-serving act for the partners but a fundamental responsibility required to be a reliable, long-term steward to *all* stakeholders. Being a good steward to your internal stakeholders (Tier One) will effectively separate a one-generational sole proprietorship model from a business that is, or can be, more profitable, investable, valuable, and durable—a significant course correction and the reason this book centers on this important stewardship element.

The principles and practices of stewardship. There are certain common core principles and practices that distinguish a small business that is a consistent, focused, long-term steward to its external stakeholders:

1. A stated, meaningful purpose (in addition to making money)

2. Fair, ethical treatment of all stakeholders

3. A commitment to quality and good service

4. The ability of the business to constantly innovate, adapt, and improve

5. A culture of continuity from one generation to the next

A principled small business is one that operates with integrity, fairness, and accountability at its core, regardless of who is watching. It is guided by clearly held values that shape every decision, from how it treats employees and customers to how it prices its products, selects its suppliers, and defines success. Being principled doesn't mean being perfect; it means being honest, consistent, and committed to doing what is right, even when it's not the easiest or most profitable path in the short term. These principles are not slogans on a wall or marketing pitches you might read in a newspaper or magazine; they are lived behaviors that earn trust, strengthen reputation, and form the foundation for lasting success.

"Never doubt that a small group of thoughtful, committed citizens can change the world. Indeed, it is the only thing that ever has."

Margaret Mead
(United States)

Being a good steward for all of your stakeholders requires consistency and focus over many years. The duration factor is what being a good steward to your internal stakeholders is all about. The premise here is simple, yet powerful: allowing next generation talent to buy in and invest in their future changes everything, for them and for you. How to get your team to think like owners? There is no better way than writing a check for principle and interest once a month to pay for their equity. It is the difference between caring about your leased apartment versus caring about the home you just signed a mortgage on. There really is no comparison.

As a prequel to what you'll learn in Part Two, "Finding 'the Extra' to Share," let's do some basic math and provide a concrete example of a multi-owner, multi-generational small business built to last. Rather than an ownership percentage structure of 50/50 for two founding owners, I advocate in this book for a percentage ownership structure, achieved over time, of 40/40/10/10, with the first two places held by the founding and senior owners who each sell 10 percent of their equity to next generation buyers, often key employees. All of a sudden, your key employees, perhaps some of your officers and/or managers, are owners! This is a force that can change the world for generations to come, propelling your business to higher growth and profitability by a team supporting one purpose. The best way to think like an owner is to be an investor and an active employee at the same time. All of this is the start of being a good steward at the Tier One level.

A small business, as we are using the term in this book and as defined more precisely in Section 1.4, is indeed unique. Unlike a larger and/or publicly traded business which can easily devote a small portion of its existing cash flow to one cause or another, small businesses can't really do that—at least not on a consistent basis. To this end, and it bears repeating, I am generally assuming that being a good steward to all of your stakeholders describes a business that has *extra* to share with its stakeholders. Finding this extra is why I advocate for starting with Tier One stakeholders while also looking after your customers or clients.

The sheer number of small businesses around the world is one thing; gently and gradually increasing the strength of each individual small business is quite another. Effectively, the argument I am making is that being a good steward, starting with your internal stakeholders, amplifies the force for change experienced by your external stakeholders and can extend it by decades. That, *plus the number of small businesses around the world*, is the difference maker. And if you still prefer to remain a *force of one* after reading this book, more power to you. I will share some ideas on how you can change the world with the business model you have for as long as you can. If you are brave enough to start and run a small business, you can help change the world as well!

STEWARDSHIP SPOTLIGHT

TONY'S CHOCOLONELY (AMSTERDAM, NETHERLANDS): Tony's Chocolonely is a Dutch chocolate manufacturer and seller founded in 2005 in Amsterdam. The company's mission is not just to eliminate exploitation within its own operations, but to drive systemic change across the global cocoa industry. Teun van de Keuken, a Dutch journalist and activist (who adopted the English name "Tony"), founded and named the company following his often lonely efforts to expose inequality and abuse in chocolate production.

Tony's purposefully sources cocoa from Ghana and Côte d'Ivoire, where more than 60 percent of the world's cocoa is grown—and where some of the industry's most serious labor and environmental challenges remain. In these two countries alone, over 1.5 million children are involved in cocoa-related child labor, and an estimated 30,000 people are victims of forced labor. Tens of thousands of hectares of tropical forest have also been cleared for cocoa production since 2019.

Tony's Chocolonely commits 1 percent of its net revenue annually to the Chocolonely Foundation, supporting projects aimed at ending systemic exploitation in the cocoa supply chain.

1.4 THE POWER OF INTEGRATED STEWARDSHIP

I REMEMBER STRUGGLING THROUGH FRENCH II my high school freshman year. I had an excellent memory, but I didn't seem to be understanding the material as well as the best students. Searching for a quick and simple solution, I compared notes with a fellow student who seemed to have a knack for foreign languages. I couldn't understand how she could translate the words she heard in French back into English, and vice versa, in her mind so quickly and easily. She looked at me like I was crazy and then explained that she didn't make any such translation. She heard the words in French and *understood* them, just like when we spoke English (or any other language, she added). I knew then that I was doomed. Memorizing allowed me to go through the motions for a while, but it wasn't a way to ever master the subject matter.

Most small businesses and their owners will need to use the two-tier approach to gradually become good stewards to all their stakeholders. This is the normal approach because most of us start a business first, figure out how to make a living, and then elect to integrate stewardship practices later. This happens sequentially *after* the business has had a chance to grow and get stronger and support the founder or founding owners. Little by little, the external stakeholders, in addition to the customers, are focused on and prioritized as the business allows and generates "its extra" time, money, and resources.

Fully integrating both tiers of stewardship could easily take years to accomplish. The point is that once accomplished, stewardship becomes as normal as turning the lights on in the morning. You see, taking care of your stakeholders isn't just about doing something more often than not, when a need arises, or when you have the time and the money. Integrated stewardship becomes fully woven into the culture or DNA of your business—not as a task to check off, but as a way of thinking, deciding, and leading. At some point, you no longer have to make the translation; it is understood. Just as a healthy business lives and breathes its mission, vision and purpose through every decision, a steward-led business lives its values in everything it does. This is the aspect of being consistent:

FOCUS + **CONSISTENCY** + DURATION = GOOD STEWARDSHIP

Integrated stewardship in the context of our two-tier stakeholder model signifies a holistic and interconnected approach where the principles and practices of stewardship are applied consistently and in a coordinated manner across both internal and external groups. This isn't just about blending the two tiers and finishing that part of the job. Integrated stewardship is a way of being in business, not just a set of things a business does or did.

This level of stewardship is about creating a business that is both *profitable and purposeful*. For most of us, this is a two-tiered process, but that isn't the only way or even the best way in every case. For a select few, the initial business plans call for a fully integrated approach from day one, such as what Bombas did. Their "buy one, donate one" concept was part of the original business plan from their inception in 2013. The founders were inspired to start Bombas after learning that socks are the most requested item in homeless shelters. Their core mission from the outset was to create a very comfortable and durable sock and then donate one for every pair sold. They sold this concept to their investors and then sold it to their customers and other stakeholders. These founders still had to build a business, of course, and profitability takes time and cash flow, among other things. Still, their focus was clear from the very start:

FOCUS + CONSISTENCY + DURATION = GOOD STEWARDSHIP

The point is that you need to find your purpose, your cause, and then focus *your extra* (time, money, services or products, knowledge, energy, know-how) accordingly. Start small, and start slow, with a clear focus, and ensure that you can be consistent in your current stewardship efforts before thinking about increasing how much you share or widening your focus to include a greater number of people or organizations. You'll find your own way once you get started. A written Stewardship Plan is a tremendous help (see Section 3.1).

It isn't that Bombas shares their *extra* time, money, or the products that they produce; extra is irrelevant to their mission. This company's creation was centered on changing the world in their chosen and well-planned way, and to also make a profit for their investors. They integrated stewardship into the foundations of their business for all of their stakeholders. I raise this point only as a learning opportunity. No small business owner reading this needs to stop what they're doing and go back and start over and reimagine their business and its purpose to integrate their two tiers of stewardship and serve all their stakeholders from the outset. Most of us didn't or couldn't do it that way. Instead, we can adapt and adjust our course gradually as to each stakeholder in each tier until they can be fully integrated over time. Doing this within a mature business with experienced owners and leaders can be a real advantage.

"We make a living by what we get, but we make a life by what we give."

Attributed to Winston Churchill
(England)

For most small businesses, building the foundations of profitability, value, and growth (mostly Tier One goals) will be the higher priority task; survival demands it. Supporting the external stakeholders such as one's community, the environment, and maintaining a proper and supportive supply chain may have to wait. Once the business is stronger and you find your extra time, money, and talent, then put your plan into motion and start to change the world with your small business. This is where integration occurs.

There is no right or wrong, or better or worse pacing as to this process. Reconciling the two tiers of stewardship and the overall needs of your small business requires a bit of a balancing act, at least in terms of prioritizing your resources. As your business resets its foundations, you will need to gradually integrate the second tier stakeholders and goals until both become a normal, natural part of your workplace. Organizing and implementing the first tier of stewardship is covered in Part Two; the second tier is mostly covered in Part Three.

The point is that most small businesses cannot and should not take on the responsibilities of stewardship to all of their stakeholders at once. There is only so much time, money, and energy to go around. This is certainly true if your small business doesn't have outside investors or private equity behind it. Prioritize being a good steward of your internal stakeholders, Tier One, along with the clients you serve. Without a solid base of operations, a clear mission and vision moving forward, and a business that can attract, reward, and retain sufficient employee talent and skills, taking your customer service and client services to new heights is nearly impossible.

Don't think of your internal stewardship goals and your external stewardship goals as in competition with each other. You should do both, but first things first. Get your house in order and take care of your customer base first.

As a fellow small business owner who started small and grew bigger over time, I am a proponent of getting specific and staying practical. You will need a plan to guide your efforts and those of your team. Your Stewardship Plan might be a formal, business plan type of document. It also might be a combination of a mission/vision statement, a legal pad on which you lay out your intentions and thoughts, and/or a detailed spreadsheet which can be used for more than just adding up columns of numbers. Whatever works for you. There are two rules: one, write down the specifics, and two, adapt your realities to the plan as it unfolds and your business grows. More instructions and specifics as to your Stewardship Plan are provided in Part Three of this book, along with suggested and well-coordinated governance provisions; effectively, documenting stewardship as you see fit into your company's DNA from one generation to the next.

Whatever your Stewardship Plan is, it will have to work for you and your team while serving your client base and paying the monthly lease and meeting your payroll, without fail. As to your stakeholders, especially those in Tier Two, there are priorities to be determined. With these tasks in mind, let's explore the practicalities in more depth as you integrate Tier Two into your business model.

Prioritize based on impact and relevance. Go back to your mission/purpose/vision statement. What is most important to you and your team? For some, it might be the environment. For others, it all starts with employee well-being. Addressing homelessness, hunger, crime, or education in your community might also be a priority. Determine which stakeholders demand the most immediate priority and what your business is capable of consistently supporting, or when it will be capable. In many cases, such a determination depends on what your business does, how mature it is, and even where it is located.

Practically, you cannot do everything in year one of your Stewardship Plan, but you might be able to do everything on your list over five years powered by a business that grows larger and stronger over that time. Using stewardship to attract and add a second generation of talent and energy to your business will enable your Stewardship Plan to come alive! It's not about how quickly you can launch your Stewardship Plan, but how well you can build it into the long-term fabric of your business. Stewardship done fast fades fast. Stewardship done well lasts a lifetime, or more.

Plan and implement your stewardship goals incrementally. Start small. Don't try to overhaul everything at once or change your corner of the world in a year or two. Choose one or two key areas to focus on initially. Break your ten-year goals down into smaller, achievable steps, revisit your Stewardship Plan annually, and put the foundations in place over time with help from your team and even your clients. Look for ways to integrate stewardship principles into your existing business processes.

Leverage your existing resources and use your limited resources to guide your goals, your near-term and long-term priorities. Involve your stakeholders, from employees to clients to suppliers. Tell them what you are doing and why. Begin by donating time and energy; monetary commitments can wait until your business is stronger and your goals are clear. Partner with local nonprofits, community groups, or industry associations. Limited resources are not so much a hinderance as they are a commonality and an opportunity to sharpen your focus. Encourage employees to contribute ideas and participate in stewardship initiatives.

Stewardship takes practice and skill, time and patience—and a good plan. Regardless, the day will come when being a good steward on behalf of all your stakeholders will become natural and seamless, if you're open to it and just... stay... with it. Perfection is not the goal. There is just the work to be done in the meantime. Small business owners are good that way.

STEWARDSHIP SPOTLIGHT

SALT SPRING COFFEE (RICHMOND, BRITISH COLUMBIA, CANADA): In 1996, founders Mickey McLeod and Robbyn Scott opened a coffee roasting café on Salt Spring Island with the mission of bringing sustainable coffee to their island community. This small business became one of Canada's early adopters of Fair Trade Certification. Since committing to fair trade, Salt Spring Coffee has contributed millions in premiums, which are additional funds paid directly to coffee farmers who decide how to reinvest the money within their own communities.

This business actively supports local community initiatives on Salt Spring Island and beyond. They often donate coffee and funds to local events, schools, and nonprofit organizations. In 2010, Salt Spring Coffee became B Corp Certified.

In 2024, the Salt Spring Coffee team partnered with the Regenerative Organic Alliance and coffee producers to launch Canada's first Regenerative Organic Certified® coffee. Regenerative organic certification sets the highest global standard for soil health, ecosystem preservation, and farmworker fairness. Guided by a deep commitment to sustainability, Mickey and Robbyn continue to pursue their vision of making the world a better place for generations to come through regenerative agriculture.

1.5 THE NEED FOR DURABILITY AND LONG-TERM SUCCESS

Imagine that one day in the future, with the help of Artificial Intelligence (AI), it is possible and common to predict one's lifespan with at least 60 percent accuracy, excluding accidents and natural disasters. Supported with accompanying medical advances, you learn that you are predicted to reach the age of 110 years, at the upper edge of what is possible at the time, and about 30 to 40 years longer than someone born today in many parts of the world. You smile. And then you start to think about the possibilities and the opportunities.

If you knew today that you might have an extra 30 to 40 years of time to work with, what would you do differently?

Maybe you don't have to wait. Many small businesses are like that today, or they could be, or should be. If you are the owner of a small, privately held business and you construct a multi-owner, multi-generational business, it can and should last for two generations or more. This is the point of learning to be a good steward of your Tier One stakeholders. Entity structures are built to outlast their human owners. It means that you might well have an extra 30 to 40 years to work with, plan with, and make a difference with. Share that with your stakeholders! This means that you have the ability to set something in motion today, even starting out as a sole proprietorship, that can make a difference fifty years from now! This is the element of duration in the stewardship formula:

FOCUS + CONSISTENCY + **DURATION** = GOOD STEWARDSHIP

I'd note that even a one generational small business can be a good steward. Ten to twenty years of focus and consistency will make a difference alongside millions of similarly situated businesses around the world. But if you purposefully build your business to outlive you, what could you do with it beyond making a good living and taking care of your family while you're alive? What could that business do for others in your community and the world in the decades to come? What would you do with that opportunity?

Before further exploring the benefits and the need for greater small business durability and long-term success, let's add some context—and a dose of reality. The scale of small businesses and their impact on society are truly staggering. According to World Bank estimates, there are **over 500 million** Micro-, Small-, and Medium-sized Enterprises (MSMEs) in developing countries/economies (a term typically focused on GDP, infrastructure, and employment) alone. Including developed economies, the global total very likely exceeds 500 million–that's a best guess of a moving, difficult to track target.

In many emerging markets (a subset of developing countries/economies), SMEs account for **about 70 percent** of formal employment and **create the majority of new jobs**. Globally, SMEs are responsible for **60 to 70 percent of employment** and contribute **around 50 percent of global GDP**, according to the United Nations and the International Federation of Accountants. The McKinsey Global Institute adds that MSMEs represent **more than 90 percent of all businesses** worldwide. In developed economies, including the United States and the European Union, SMEs account for **over 99 percent** of all registered businesses. In the U.S. alone, based on data from the Small Business Administration (SBA), the Bureau of Labor Statistics (BLS), and the Census Bureau, there are **approximately 33 million small businesses**—with **98 percent employing fewer than 100 people** and **over 80 percent having fewer than twenty total workers**.

Taken together, **half-a-billion small businesses** around the world are not just the "backbone" of the economy—*they are the economy*.

As to what constitutes a "small business," definitions vary widely across countries and industries. For the purposes of this book, we will define a small business as any enterprise with 1 to 100 total owners and employees. This range captures the heart of what most people around the world recognize as a small business—a company that remains personally led, closely held, and deeply rooted in its local community. Globally, businesses of this size are responsible for the majority of job creation, innovation, and economic vitality. Although some official definitions classify businesses with up to 250 or even 500 employees as "small," this broader range often reflects the needs of industrial sectors or government programs. For our focus on stewardship and owner-driven success, 1 to 100 people reflects the size where personal leadership, long-term vision, and community connection matter most. And if your business employs 150, 200, or 500 people, I won't be offended if you keep reading. We can learn from each other.

Despite the impressive totals above, starting and running a new small business is challenging under the best of circumstances. To better understand the risks, we can look at data from the BLS which, while based on U.S. businesses, offers a useful benchmark for small businesses around the world. Here's what the numbers show:

- About **20 percent** of new businesses fail within their first **two years**.

- Around **45 percent** fail within **five years**.

- Approximately **65 percent** fail within **ten years**.

Think about that: **nearly two-thirds of new small businesses will not survive to celebrate their tenth anniversary.**

Before moving forward, it is worth pausing to revisit the role of data and its accuracy in this discussion. Numbers are an essential part of the story. Tracking the revenue and profitability of a Fortune 500 company+ is relatively straightforward as public companies are required to publish audited financial reports; small businesses are not. That is how the system is structured. As a result, businesses with 1 to 100 owners and employees—which make up the overwhelming majority of enterprises globally—are markedly underrepresented in academic research, reporting frameworks, and public discourse. Despite their significant contributions to employment and economic activity, small businesses are often overlooked in favor of larger, more visible corporations. This lack of representation can create the misleading perception that small businesses are less sophisticated and less impactful. This is a critical error.

Small business entrepreneurs bring optimism, resilience, and energy to their work— qualities that are difficult to quantify through traditional data collection methods. Attitude, perseverance, and local economic vitality are not easily measured, but their importance cannot be overstated. Small businesses should not, and must not, allow themselves to be marginalized. Collectively, they represent a force capable of driving significant change. The path to that impact begins by stewarding their businesses, people, and communities with intention and care.

Why does time, or a small business's durability, matter in the context of stewardship and doing good for others? It's not like a new, small business with a caring and determined owner can't make a difference in their community as a good steward *while still in business*. From my own experience, I would argue that it is exceedingly difficult for a small business and its owner(s) to focus on being a force for positive change on more than an occasional basis when trying to make a living from one day to the next. It can be an all-consuming process to nurture a small business, whether in the end it succeeds or fails.

Sole proprietorships are the most common type of small business—and for good reason. They are simple and quick to set up, nimble and adaptable once under-way, and capable of filling a gap or addressing a need in the marketplace almost overnight. They can easily support a small staff and a payroll. However, they also typically do not last beyond the working career of their founding owner—and often much less, as BLS data suggests. Depending on the data source, it is clear that in the United States, roughly 70 to 75 percent of all small businesses are structured as sole proprietorships, including a significant number of single-member LLCs that file tax returns as sole proprietors. Worldwide, I would expect the proportion of sole proprietorships to be similar, if not even higher.

When it comes to changing the world through a small business, there is nothing to stop a single owner from making a difference, especially in a cumulative sense. Sole proprietors are some of the hardest working and most creative people I've ever met. They have my full respect. The challenge is that while all small businesses have limited resources, a sole proprietorship is arguably *more limited* than most other small businesses in terms of capital, time, cash flow and efficiency, and staffing. In addition, it takes years, even a decade or more, for most new sole proprietorships to reach a point of being financially stable or viable where there is extra money or assets to share in terms of stewardship. These hardworking solo owners may have almost immeasurable energy, drive, and courage, but most of these attributes are centered on making a living and serving clients. They have to grow in every respect to generate *the extra* to be good stewards to all of their stakeholders.

For small businesses with ten to twenty employees (owners included), it still takes time, effort, and resilience to find their footing. Even then, most don't last more than ten years as the statistics reveal. Too many small businesses get caught in what I call *the Founder's Treadmill*—the setup-struggle-grow-stall pattern that leads to early burnout or closure. You run faster and faster as the grade becomes steeper and steeper, and then all your energy is gone. New businesses spring up to take your place, and the cycle simply repeats. What if we could change that pattern? What if more small businesses could not only survive, but endure—growing stronger, more valuable, and more rooted in the communities they serve?

If we could measurably reduce failure rates by strengthening small businesses both mechanically, through better structures and operations, and philosophically through intentional, professional stewardship practices, each small business could make a bigger impact, sooner, and for much longer. This durable business path could be the difference maker.

Too idealistic? Perhaps. But remember: there are approximately 500 million micro-, small-, and medium-sized businesses worldwide. A shift of even one percent would mean **5 million additional** stronger, self-sufficient, viable small businesses—each better equipped to support its stakeholders and communities for another decade or more. Given the resilience and hard work that define this particular business group, I suspect we can aim even higher.

Interestingly, even among the more successful small businesses, most survive only one generation at best. Having spent thirty years working on these issues, I think that a big part of the problem may lie in an imbalance—too much taken, too little given back—and a lack of practical business strengthening steps around equity ownership and stewardship. By adding in a good succession plan, that extra decade becomes an extra generation. These problems are solvable, at least for some small businesses.

Small business owners who want to be good stewards to all of their stakeholders have some issues to address. To this end, the entire middle section of this book (Part Two, *Finding 'The Extra' to Share*) is intended to put a significant dent in the one-generational sole prop model and the high failure rates of new, small businesses and, perhaps, inexperienced owners.

There are hundreds, if not thousands, of relatively current self-help and/or subscriber-oriented business building books on the market today in a wide variety of languages. There are also a lot of coaches offering to help small business owners figure it out. And yet, failure rates are sky high. I'd like you to think of being a good Tier One steward as a new gear in this process where we shift our focus to ownership or equity as the means, the motivator, and the solution for building durable, long(er)-lasting small businesses. We don't have to save every entrepreneur, but if we can substantially strengthen the ones that can be saved, they can make a meaningful difference for generations to come. This is doable.

I've written five nonfiction books on business perpetuation, succession planning, and durability of small businesses. It works. It matters. As for what's in it for you along the way? Durability and long-term success, even as you work to achieve those goals, also translates to:

- **Increased Business Value:** Sustained profitability and growth make a business more attractive to potential buyers or investors, leading to higher equity value.

- **Brand Equity and Customer Loyalty:** Established businesses with a proven track record benefit from stronger brand recognition and customer loyalty, contributing to long-term stability. A multi-generational client base is also possible.

- **Learning and Improvement:** Years of operation provide valuable insights and experience, shared with next generation owners and key employees, allowing for continuous improvement and adaptation to market changes.

- **Intergenerational Wealth Transfer:** A long-lasting business can be passed down to future generations, creating a lasting legacy and potential for continued wealth creation. You will have more options.

Simply stated, a mature business with a trained, experienced staff and loyal, devoted clientele can share more of its resources (time, profits, goodwill, knowledge, etc.) in whatever manner it chooses, consistently, with its stakeholders for a longer time. Seriously consider that the stakeholders who initially benefit from a Tier One focus are internal to the business—you, your family, your fellow owners, your key employees. When 50 million of these even slightly stronger, mature businesses and their well-motivated owners around the world weigh in, we really can change the world. Stewardship is an investment in strength and endurance.

STEWARDSHIP SPOTLIGHT

ECOFLOW (SHENZHEN, CHINA), was founded in 2017 by a cross-border team of four young entrepreneurs—two American and two Chinese. Based in Shenzhen, they shared a bold vision: to make clean, portable power accessible anywhere on earth. Starting with limited capital and a small team, they combined engineering talent with a deep sense of global responsibility.

From the beginning, EcoFlow's mission extended beyond profit. Their flagship solar-powered generators and battery storage systems serve outdoor enthusiasts and digital nomads, but they've also become lifelines in rural and off-grid communities, disaster zones, and areas with unreliable infrastructure.

EcoFlow's stewardship shows up in how they design for long-term durability, prioritize clean energy, and deliver practical solutions to real-world problems. Even as the company has grown, their startup DNA remains visible in their agility, innovation, and purpose-driven culture.

For small business owners around the world, EcoFlow is a reminder that great impact doesn't require a big team—just a clear mission, a commitment to sustainability, and the courage to build something the world truly needs.

1.6 MYTHS AND MISCONCEPTIONS

When it comes to small business stewardship, misinformation is everywhere. Certain ideas—that stewardship is only about charity, that it requires sacrificing profits, or that it is too complex for smaller businesses—persist despite strong evidence to the contrary. These myths not only create unnecessary hesitation but also prevent business owners from recognizing stewardship as a practical, powerful framework for long-term success; what some see as an obligation, most will see as an opportunity. In this section, we will debunk some of the most common misconceptions and show how true stewardship is both accessible and essential for any small business committed to growth and making a lasting impact.

Myth: **Stewardship is about giving things away.**

Reality: Stewardship is about managing all business resources—people, profit, influence, opportunity—wisely and responsibly for the benefit of others *and* the long-term health of the business. But many people do equate stewardship with generosity in the form of donations, volunteering, or giving things away for free. While generosity can be one expression of stewardship, it is not the core of it. This misconception paints stewardship as a soft, one-directional act of benevolence that is usually unsustainable for a small business.

Stewardship in small business is not about giving things away—it is about *managing what you have responsibly* on behalf of your internal (Tier One) and ex-ternal (Tier Two) stakeholders. It is about long-term thinking, protecting and improving resources (not just redistributing them), and ensuring that all stakeholders—employees, customers, suppliers, communities, and even the business itself—are treated with care and foresight. Stewardship involves de-cisions that balance purpose and profitability so the business becomes more durable, valuable, and impactful over time. It is not about a one-way gifting process. It is a disciplined practice of making sure that all of what you are re-sponsible for today can still serve and thrive tomorrow.

Myth: **Any charitable act is stewardship.**

Reality: While charitable giving can be admirable, it is not automatically stewardship. Good stewardship requires intentional, strategic action aimed at long-term benefit. Simply donating surplus goods or funds may feel good, but without addressing or at least being aware of root causes, such efforts can create dependency, disrupt local economies, or overlook more sustainable solutions. A well-thought out Stewardship Plan (see Section 3.1) can help a small business develop the best approach over time.

Take Elvis & Kresse, a U.K.-based company that rescues decommissioned fire hoses and transforms them into luxury accessories. Instead of seeing these materials dumped into a landfill, they have built an entire business model around environmental stewardship and circular design. And even their charitable giving is strategic—they donate 50% of profits from their fire hose line to the Fire Fighters Charity, ensuring ongoing support for first responders in a way that grows as their business grows.

Myth: **Stewardship is primarily about minimizing or tightly controlling profits.**

Reality: There are pundits who think this way, but this perspective is usually aimed at larger, even publicly owned businesses. A good steward considers the long-term impact of their decisions, not just short-term profits. And stewardship encompasses a much broader set of values including ethical conduct, fair treatment of stakeholders, social responsibility, and a commitment to quality and service. That said, small businesses also must be sufficiently profitable to attract next-generation ownership and talent; profits are how next gen owners pay for the equity they acquire, and it is a big part of why they buy in. Profitability is what determines the value of a small business, so minimizing it is rarely the goal of an owner working towards being a good steward. In this book, the goal is teach you how to maximize your growth and profitability in order to be a better steward to all of your stakeholders.

Myth: **To be a good steward, one must serve *all* stakeholders.**

Reality: Yes, that is the job. I do not believe that you have to serve all of your stakeholders equally or with the same level of priority—that depends on your purpose and your goals. As I look over the list of stakeholders, however, I cannot imagine not serving them all well in a business built to grow and make the world a better place. I do think that writing out your mission statement and memorializing your preferences and intentions (i.e., a formal Stewardship Plan and adjusting your supporting governance provisions—see Sections 3.1 and 3.2) is smart and will help you better address your stakeholder's needs with the extra you can share.

Part of the formula advocated for in this book is a focus on a narrower group of organizations within your stakeholders. Some successful small businesses share their extra with hundreds of nonprofit organizations and other recipients who need support. That's wonderful, but not practical for most small business owners trying to make a living. You can take care of all your stakeholders, make a significant difference, and still maintain a relatively narrow focus if you plan carefully and adapt over time.

Myth: **Visible generosity equals meaningful impact.**

Reality: Just because a business is *seen* doing good does not mean it is creating lasting value. Stewardship is measured by outcomes over time, not optics.

Myth: **Stewardship is only for large corporations with complex structures.**

Reality: The principles of stewardship are applicable to businesses of all sizes. In a small business, it might manifest itself as the owner leading by example, fostering a positive work environment, embracing one or more local charities or nonprofit organizations, creating an ownership track for younger, key employees, and ensuring ethical practices are followed daily. Large corporations not only have more complex structures, they often have many investors, officers, and/or board members to report to. Small businesses have short, efficient decision-chains and are often face-to-face with their stakeholders. I would argue that small businesses are much better suited for the role of stewardship and changing the world than larger, even Fortune 500 companies+.

Myth: **Small businesses do not have the resources to prioritize stakeholder needs beyond customers and employees.**

Reality: Ironically, in authoring this book, I have assumed that to be the case for many of the smallest businesses. The myth lies in this being an infinite statement of fact or a reason not to improve and find *your extra*. While resources can be a constraint, many small businesses are deeply embedded in their local communities and can help in other ways. Their owners often have direct, personal relationships with customers, suppliers, neighbors, employees, and even competitors. This allows for a more informal but often highly effective form of stakeholder stewardship. A small business, led by its owner(s), might volunteer time or materials to local charities, participate in community events, or offer personalized service in ways larger corporations cannot. This inherent connection often drives small business leaders to consider and address stakeholder needs even without dedicated departments or a large budget.

Myth: **Small business stewardship also includes the goal of doing no (additional) harm to the environment or one's community.**

Reality: I categorize this notion as a myth if "doing no additional harm" is your primary goal, and it stops there. It is okay to include this initial goal, but as a part of a broader, perhaps short-term plan. Good stewardship is a proactive, forward-looking series of long-term, consistent actions that align with a small business's purpose and goals. Yes, changing directions on a given issue might involve a point in time where your small business stops moving in the wrong direction, pivots, and starts moving in a better or proper direction, but your Stewardship Plan, your core principles, and your purpose need to be positive and not just neutral. No one said that changing the world would be easy!

Myth: **The owner is the boss and can do whatever they want.**

Reality: It is good to be king (or queen), but the Tier One stakeholders require full support as well. While small business owners have significant autonomy, being a good steward involves recognizing one's responsibilities to employees, the business/entity, officers and managers, even one's fellow owners. It is not just about personal gain but about the well-being and sustainability of the business ecosystem. If a business has an ownership group of one and that never changes, the business will die or be acquired. Smart owners are good leaders who care about their stakeholders and are always prepared for whatever the future may bring; best accomplished with a strong, diverse team.

Myth: **Steward-Ownership is the same as being a good steward.**

Reality: The term "steward-ownership" is not the same thing as being a good steward, but is an important concept to be familiar with. Start by considering that the owner(s) or shareholder(s) of a small business commonly own both the economic rights and the control rights. Steward-ownership refers to the process whereby these rights are purposefully and legally separated, which is something you might see in a larger, more successful small business (around 100 employees or more) or a business that is purposely set up with this control mechanism on start-up before seeking outside investment. In such an instance, control over the business is literally placed in the hands of stewards—individuals or groups whose job is to protect the business's mission and core values from one generation to the next. But there is a catch, in a good way.

These stewards are not allowed to sell their decision-making rights, nor can they profit personally from their ability to exert control, ensuring that the business remains aligned with its stated purpose. Investors can still provide financial support and receive fair returns, but they do not get to dictate the direction of the business. By cutting the link between power and financial gain, companies are free to focus on what truly matters to them—making a positive impact.

Myth: **Succession planning only matters when the owner is ready to retire.**

Reality: Responsible stewardship includes planning for the future of the ownership and leadership of the business, even if, especially if, retirement is ten years away. A professional, practical succession plan involves a series of gradual next gen equity purchases over time and can easily require ten to twenty years to properly transition from one generation to another, while continuing to be good stewards of all the stakeholders. Having a detailed plan in place, well in advance, whether it's identifying potential successors within the family or the business, or considering an eventual sale, is crucial for the long-term viability of the enterprise and the protection of its value. You can learn more about this process in Part Two.

If you would like to read more, I previously published the only up-to-date series of succession planning books for each generation of ownership: *Building With the End in Mind* for current owners, and *Acquiring Your Future Through a Succession Plan* for next generation ownership prospects, available on Amazon and through many other popular book distributors.

Myth: **Bringing in outside equity (investors) means losing control and is therefore poor stewardship.**

Reality: While bringing in outside equity can dilute or reset ownership, it can also be a responsible act of stewardship if it provides the necessary capital for growth, innovation, scalability, or to overcome financial challenges. Outside equity or investment might ultimately secure the long-term future of a business, benefiting all stakeholders. The key is to carefully consider the terms and the alignment of interests with the new investors. Well-documented governance provisions can help to ensure continuity in a business's stewardship goals. Steward-ownership provisions, addressed above, might also be utilized.

Myth: **A small business's entity structure does not really matter as long as the business is growing and profitable.**

Reality: A complete myth! The chosen ownership structure (sole proprietorship, LLC/partnership, LLC/DE, S corporation, C corporation, etc.) has significant implications for liability, taxation, profitability, investment, and the transferability of equity or ownership. Responsible stewardship involves understanding these implications and choosing the structure that best suits the business's current and future needs, including potential exit strategies before the business grows too large. A sole proprietorship is a one-generational model, if that, and does not accommodate next generation investment. Your business entity structure is like the foundation of your dream home—it supports everything built on top of it.

Myth: **The owner's family is automatically entitled to take over the business, regardless of their capabilities.**

Reality: The short answer is, not necessarily. While family succession is a common goal for many small business owners, being a good Tier One steward involves a thoughtful and objective assessment of whether family members have the necessary skills, passion, and commitment to lead the business effectively. Sometimes, the best act of stewardship is to look outside the family for at least some of the next generation leaders and/or owners, a model often characterized as a *family-like* business. Next generation prospective owners or active investors should definitely perform thorough due diligence on this issue and read through the governance documents and buy-sell provisions to determine who the successors will be and how they are selected. An absence of such documentation means that the business has not properly prepared for such events.

STEWARDSHIP SPOTLIGHT

LITTLE YELLOW BIRD (WELLINGTON, NEW ZEALAND) This small clothing company is setting a new standard for sustainability. Little Yellow Bird uses 100 percent organic and sustainably grown cotton. They then weave and dye the cotton using low-impact techniques that conserve water and energy. Their products, mostly workwear, are manufactured in factories that adhere to ethical standards, including fair wages, safe working conditions, and no forced or child labor.

But the company does not stop there. Little Yellow Bird's circularity program ensures that its clothing does not end up in landfills at the end of its lifespan. In fact, they even accept clothing from other brands. The clothes get sorted by condition and are either resold, donated, or downcycled into items such as dog beds. Clothing beyond repair is broken down and recycled into new fabrics. In 2021, Little Yellow Bird was recognized as a "Best for the World" B Corp, which placed them in the top 5 percent of all B Corps for their overall impact on workers, community, customers, and the environment.

1.7 CONSIDERING THE B CORPORATION MODEL

THE CONCEPT OF THE B Corporation® was started by a nonprofit organization called B Lab in 2006. Certified B Corporations, or B Corps, are companies verified by B Lab to meet high standards of social and environmental performance, transparency, and accountability. B Lab reports a global community of **over 8,400 Certified B Corporations** across **96 countries**, employing **more than 750,000 workers** in **162 industries**.

Simple division suggests that this equates to approximately **90 workers per B Corp**, which, on average, places these businesses well within our working definition of a small business. Over time, it will be interesting to observe whether the emphasis shifts toward ramping up the number of certified businesses and maintaining accessibility, or setting a higher barrier to entry to create a more exclusive group of certified companies.

B Lab and B Corps' stated global vision is to create an inclusive, equitable, and regenerative economic system for all people and the planet. Website text speaks of mobilizing the B Corp movement to change our economic system—not just in the U.S. or Europe, but globally—to positively impact all stakeholders including workers, communities, customers, and the planet. And they add a promise that "We won't stop until all business is a force for good." For me as an author, and for you as a reader of this book, thinking big and beyond ourselves is likely why our respective paths are crossing at this moment in time.

There are certainly other organizations that offer businesses certification or verification as well, each with its own standards and qualifications. Some of the better known groups are the Fair Trade Federation, Fair for Life, Green Business Certification, and the Social Enterprise World Forum. Still others are listed under the "Important Notes" section in the front of this book. The goal in this specific section, however, is to study a specific example—how a B Corp is certified and what it takes to be a B Corp—and to learn from the process and apply some of the thinking to your own small business. While not all stewardly businesses are B Corps, this certification provides a framework and external validation of your commitment, certainly something to consider on behalf of your stakeholders.

B Lab believes that businesses need comprehensive, credible, comparable impact standards to support economic systems change. B Lab was founded with the idea that a different kind of economy is not only possible, it is necessary—and that businesses, of all types and sizes around the world, can lead the way towards a new, stakeholder-driven model. As a certified B Corporation and as a leader of this new, emerging economy, the specific set of beliefs are these:

- That we must be the change we seek in the world

- That all business ought to be conducted as if people and place mattered

- That, through their products, practices, and profits, businesses should aspire to do no harm and to benefit all

- To do so requires that we act with the understanding that we are each dependent upon another and thus responsible for each other and future generations

B Corps are required to undergo a rigorous evaluation (called the B Impact Assessment) as to their impact on their stakeholders. B Corps must legally commit to safeguarding the interests of *all* stakeholders, not just shareholders, and demonstrate transparency in their operations. The B Impact Assessment evaluates a company's practices and outputs across these five categories:

- Governance

- Workers

- Community

- Environment

- Customers

According to B Corp rules, a business's stakeholders are defined broadly to include all individuals or groups who have an interest in the company's operations and outcomes. By substituting "shareholders/investors" for "governance" in the list above, you will have a B Corp's basic list of stakeholders.

B Corp certification requires not only an initial assessment by B Lab but also ongoing verification every three years to ensure that a certified business continues to live up to its commitments. This process is intended to create accountability for responsible practices. B Corps are also required to make their impact data publicly available, fostering transparency and trust with customers, employees, and the community. This allows for outside parties to ensure that the company is keeping its word and fulfilling its stewardship responsibilities.

"We are born with obligations, not rights."

Carlos Fuentes
(Mexico)

B Lab does not impose a minimum or maximum size requirement on a business interested in certification. This means that very small businesses, including sole proprietorships, can become B Corp certified. In fact, to their credit, B Lab provides specific guidance for small enterprises, recognizing that the certification process may present unique challenges for this group. B Lab also has a small enterprise guide for businesses that generate less than $10M USD in annual revenue and employ fewer than fifty full-time employees. B Corp certification is primarily focused on a company's social and environmental impact, not its size.

As leaders in the movement for economic systems change, B Corps have an opportunity to reap some important benefits in return. Such certified businesses can build trust with consumers, communities, and suppliers; attract and retain like-minded employees; and draw mission-aligned investors. Due to the ongoing verification process, B Corps tend to be focused on continuous improvement, leading to their long-term resilience. As you are learning, being a good steward for your stakeholders requires consistency and focus over many years; this is how the B Corp model does it.

B Corp certification is said to be holistic, not exclusively focused on a single social or environmental issue. And the process to achieve and maintain certification often requires engaging teams and departments across a given business if large enough. Taking company size and profile into account, verification involves documentation of your business model and information about your operations, structure, and various work processes, as well as a review of potential public complaints, and even a possible site visit. There is an annual fee to be a B Corp starting around $2,000 USD, increasing in amount based on the annual revenue of the certified business.

In terms of how the B Corp model applies to being a good steward, B Corps legally commit to considering the impact of their decisions on all of their stakeholders. This expands the definition of good stewardship well beyond maximizing profits or increasing shareholder value. The B Corp model also encourages a long-term business perspective, focusing on sustainable practices and creating a positive impact for future generations. This aligns well with the core principles of being a good Tier One steward.

One of the most interesting aspects of the B Corp model, at least in terms of being a good steward, is the need to amend a business's governing documents. This is also where the process starts to get a bit complicated for a small business, likely requiring your local attorney to assist. B Corps are required to change their corporate governance structure to be accountable to all stakeholders, not just shareholders, and achieve benefit corporation status if available in their jurisdiction. These changes are designed to ensure that a business's commitment to considering all stakeholders is legally binding on all current *and future* shareholders.

While B Corp certification represents a valuable and important effort to promote responsible business practices and is frequently mentioned in the Stewardship Spotlights at the end of every section in this book, it is not without its critics. These criticisms highlight the ongoing challenges of ensuring that certifications accurately reflect genuine social and environmental impact around the world and for many businesses. To be fair, many of these concerns apply to other organizations as well. Here are some of the key concerns:

- **Greenwashing**, where a business presents and attempts to benefit from a facade of sustainability while its underlying practices are still problematic.

- **Slacktivism** is a pejorative term that describes actions taken to appear to support a political or social cause but which require minimal personal effort and have little actual impact on achieving the cause.

- Applying **varied standards and subjectivity.**

- **Lack of stringent enforcement.**

- **Cost and accessibility**, especially for small businesses.

- **Investor concerns.** Some investors that are solely or primarily focused on maximized financial return may be put off by the B Corp structure due to the legal requirements to consider all stakeholders' interests.

- **Complexity and bureaucracy**. The B Corp certification process is known to be complex and time-consuming, perhaps a purposeful barrier to entry. But this can be a deterrent to smaller companies with limited resources.

In this section, we've explored one way, among many, to use small businesses as a force for good. Whether or not you pursue certification, the real value lies in reflecting on how your business can make a meaningful difference. Most entrepreneurs are naturally drawn to good ideas that work—and that matter.

In my thirty years as a small business owner, I never sought B Corp certification. Not because I was opposed to it, but because I didn't feel the need for someone else's stamp of approval to do right by my people or the planet. I suspect that's true for many small business owners who are too busy running lean teams and making payroll to add yet another process and responsibility, even a well-intended one.

B Lab has made a real contribution to the conversation. But here's the math: 8,400 certified B Corps in two decades. Meanwhile, there are 500 million small businesses globally. If we want to change the world, we need an approach that's simpler, faster, and more scalable. That's why this book relies on something even more powerful: your values, your integrity, and your daily choices.

The work ahead is real. It is meaningful. And it belongs to honest, hardworking business owners like you.

STEWARDSHIP SPOTLIGHT

KEEPCUP (MELBOURNE, AUSTRALIA): KeepCup was founded in 2009 with the primary goal of encouraging the reuse of coffee cups and diverting single-use cups from landfills. They provide an online tool to help individuals and businesses calculate the environmental savings of using a KeepCup compared to disposable alternatives. According to KeepCup's Life Cycle Analysis, a KeepCup Original & Brew breaks even with single-use cups after just twenty-four uses, and their Thermal range of cups after sixty-six uses.

KeepCup is a member of 1% for the Planet, committing to donate at least 1 percent of their global revenue to environmental causes. They partner with organizations like Sea Shepherd and the Plastic Free Foundation, often creating co-branded products where a portion of the revenue goes directly to support these causes. They support local community cleanups and environmental initiatives. KeepCup is a leader in the reuse revolution and has successfully diverted millions of cups from landfills each year. KeepCup is a certified B Corporation as well.

1.8 THE WORLD NEEDS YOU NOW!

THE STEWARDSHIP MOVEMENT ISN'T HAPPENING in a vacuum—it's being accelerated by a cultural and economic shift that no small business owner can afford to ignore. More than ever, customers and clients are aligning their purchasing decisions with their personal values. They're asking questions that go beyond price and product: How do you treat your employees? Where do your materials come from? Are you part of this community or just extracting from it? And technology makes the answers, or lack thereof, easier to find than ever.

This isn't just a trend. It is a long-term realignment of trust and loyalty. In the past, brand names and scale equaled credibility. Today, authenticity, transparency, and integrity carry more weight. Customers want to support businesses that reflect their values—and that's precisely where principled small business stewards shine. You don't need a billion-dollar ad budget to earn loyalty. You need to show up with purpose, consistency, and care. Integrity builds equity, even when it's not on the balance sheet. Stewardship isn't just a differentiator in this environment, it's becoming the expectation.

In this Section, I am not going to cite national or global statistics about hunger, poverty, homelessness, illiteracy, lack of water or sanitation, natural disasters, and climate change. The list of challenges and problems around the world needing our attention is long and sobering and things don't seem to be getting better on most fronts. We all know that there are plenty of problems and unmet needs out there. Find *your* cause. Develop a formal Stewardship Plan. Get your house in order, and then get started helping as you can. Share your efforts with your stakeholders and tell them how you team is making a difference. Just remember the basic formula for good small business stewardship in the course of your preparation and thinking:

FOCUS + CONSISTENCY + DURATION

These requirements separate good deeds from good stewardship. Singular, occasional actions and good deeds make us feel happy and proud but will not permanently change anything. While I hope you do feel good about your contributions, I would rather the people or groups needing and receiving your help feel good about what you have done, knowing they have not seen the last of your stewardship and that of your many small business colleagues.

Most people use the words "empathy" and "compassion" interchangeably. But in truth, there is a significant and powerful difference—one that matters a great deal in business, in life, and in stewardship:

- **Empathy** is the ability to understand someone else's experience from their perspective—even if it is different from your own.

- **Compassion** is the willingness to act on that understanding with care and intention.

Empathy connects. Compassion responds. Both are important. But the latter is the gateway to stewardship.

When you take the helm of a small business, you create a vessel that can do some amazing things. It is, or can be, a force multiplier. As others joined the small business I started, we got better over time, stronger, more resilient. We were able to adapt to a changing marketplace and could pivot quickly to take advantage of new opportunities or to avoid imminent threats. I could not have succeeded without a great team and a deep pool of talent. We were so much better together, and they made me better as an owner and leader. I learned how to do things I never thought possible. My team knew things and had talents I respected and admired.

Your small business is your superpower. Where, when, and how you use that power is an awesome responsibility. Regardless of your business size or age, wherever you are in the world and whatever your cause, you are needed because you can do things that individuals cannot, and the world needs you now. This process, of course, is entirely voluntary, but it is best thought of as volunteering at a professional level. Stewardship requires a higher level of sharing and giving. To achieve the needed consistency and duration, your business has to be team-based at some point. You will have to innovate and improve. You will have to grow and become more profitable and valuable. What got you here will not get you there. I think that is a good thing and I trust you do, too.

This book is about living a great life and using your business skills and the team you hired and work with to help others live better lives. It is also about running a better business for most, because that is necessary to be a good, consistent, *long-term* steward to your stakeholders. To reiterate, I am not suggesting for a minute that you set aside a portion of what you are currently earning. That is great if you can, but learning to be a good Tier One steward is more about building something stronger, more efficient, with more people *pulling on the oars of your vessel*, propelling it forward. Once you have your business in order and your clients are well served, look to the other external stakeholders and add them to your stewardship efforts.

So, let's get ready for the next major step in this journey: building and finding *the extra to share*.

In Part Two of this book, we will explore how to compartmentalize your business cash flows and use profitability as a guidepost to greater success. These relatively simple but effective strategies are not intended to make your business larger, but if you employ this thinking in the coming years as you grow smartly, it will help you develop a profitable, valuable, and investable business that can do more.

---

*"Rowing harder doesn't help
if the boat is headed in the wrong direction."*

Kenichi Ohmae
(Japan)

That said, there is no minimum size in terms of revenue, profits, or staffing for a principled small business to help change the world and make things better, even just a little bit at a time. Many small businesses are, well, quite small... as in one person. Every small business owner can do something, even as a force of one. My sister, Mary, runs her own pet grooming business from a spare room in her house while also taking care of a son with special needs as a single parent. She works hard, is great at what she does, and is in high demand. She is my hero. There is not much extra to go around at the end of the month, and still Mary gives back to her community by donating her time and skills to animal rescue organizations and to animals in need of a good friend, a warm bath, and a new start. She has no mission statement, no corporation or entity structure, but she most certainly has a purpose and has found a way to be a good, consistent steward in her community. Mary's small business, however, will come to an end when she retires; in the meantime, it will slow down as she does.

Adding another owner to your business, or even several owners over the next ten years, if possible and practical, changes everything. Mind you that we are talking about 5 percent to 10 percent, maybe up to 20 percent ownership stakes in most cases, per buy-in opportunity. As the founding owner(s), you will still be in control for as long as you want to be. Making a business *investable* is a skill that every founding owner who aspires to being a good steward beyond their own career must learn—we will use the middle part of this book to explain how this works. I believe in equity. The best way to learn to think like an owner is to be an owner. Note that I have placed your business/entity and you and your fellow owners near the top of the list of stakeholders. First things first.

As we conclude Part One, a bit of perspective is in order. Looking back over a thirty-year period of small business ownership, here is what I learned in terms of being a good steward of a small business and, sometimes, not being such a good steward:

a) Stay humble

b) Live within your means

c) Include each owners' family on your list of stakeholders

d) Surround yourself with great people and hold on to them

e) Hire people who are (much) better than you at a given task/role

f) Be *more generous* with internal stakeholders (time off, pay, benefits), not just *competitive*

g) Find your cause(s)—this is the "focus" part of the stewardship formula. Start by selecting just one or two community-based charities or nonprofits, stay with them, and consistently share your time and money with them. Gradually add one global charity or nonprofit and stay with them, doing more to help as you are able to.

I worked with a lot of very successful financial advisors and planners in the course of my career. These folks are professional money managers. In the course of consulting and teaching, I learned as a young owner that leveraging business operations is one thing; leveraging your lifestyle alongside a leveraged business is quite another and greatly limits one's ability to be a good steward. I came to appreciate the mindset of staying out of debt on at least one front, home or business. Debt is not a bad thing if carefully and strategically managed, but too much, on too many fronts, changes your outlook about everything, stewardship included.

Starting and running a small business with any level of success is a significant achievement of which you should be very proud. Practicing good stewardship on behalf of all your stakeholders and changing your part of the world is life changing. One day, when you retire and look back on your accomplishments and all the people whose lives you touched, this will be your story to tell. Humility aside, I hope you tell everyone!

STEWARDSHIP SPOTLIGHT

DR. BRONNER'S MAGIC SOAPS (VISTA, CALIFORNIA): According to this small business's website, Dr. Bronner's was founded in 1948 by Emanuel Bronner, a third-generation Master soap maker from a German-Jewish soapmaking family. He used the (very detailed) labels on his ecological soaps to spread his message that we must realize our unity across religious and ethnic divides: "We are All-One or None." Still family-owned and run, Dr. Bronner's honors its founder's vision by making socially and environmentally responsible products of the highest quality—and by dedicating profits to help make a better world.

Dr. Bronner's is a pioneer in ethical sourcing and actively works to ensure fair wages and working conditions for the farmers and workers in their supply chains around the world. They have established direct, fair trade relationships with producers of key ingredients like coconut oil, palm oil, olive oil, cocoa, and sugar in countries like Ghana, Sri Lanka, Samoa, Palestine, Israel, India, Ecuador, Indonesia, and Brazil. Their commitment is formalized through certifications like Fair for Life.

The company has a five-to-one cap on executive salaries, meaning Dr. Bronner's executives cannot make more than five times that of the lowest-wage, fully vested employee. Dr. Bronner's chose to drop their B Corp certification.

REFERENCES/PART ONE
(IN ALPHABETICAL ORDER):

B Lab. 2021. Best for the World Honorees. B Lab Official Website (Archive). Accessed May 14, 2025. https://bcorporation.net/programs-and-tools/best-for-the-world.

B Lab. 2025. Certified B Corporation Community: Global Impact Overview. B Lab Official Website. Accessed May 14, 2025. https://www.bcorporation.net/en-us/movement/b-corp-community/.

B Lab. 2025. Certified B Corporations Directory. B Lab Official Website. Accessed May 14, 2025. https://bcorporation.net/directory/king-arthur-baking-company-inc.

Bombas LLC. 2024. Impact Report. Bombas Official Website. Accessed May 14, 2025. https://bombas.com/pages/impact.

Burberry Foundation. 2017. Burberry Foundation Partners with Elvis & Kresse to Tackle Leather Waste. Burberry Group PLC Press Release. Accessed May 14, 2025. https://www.burberryplc.com/en/news/burberry-foundation-and-elvis-and-kresse-partnership.html.

ECOALF. 2025. Our Commitment: Because There Is No Planet B. ECOALF Official Website. Accessed May 14, 2025. https://ecoalf.com/en/pages/ecoalf-our-commitment.

ECOALF. 2025. Our Mission and Sustainability Commitments. ECOALF Official Website. Accessed May 14, 2025. https://ecoalf.com/en/pages/our-mission.

EcoFlow. "About Us." Accessed May 20, 2025. https://www.ecoflow.com/us/about-us

Elvis & Kresse. 2025. Our Story: Rescuing Materials, Transforming Lives. Elvis & Kresse Official Website. Accessed May 14, 2025. https://www.elvisandkresse.com/pages/our-story.

European Commission, Annual Report on European SMEs 2023/2024, accessed May 13, 2025, https://single-market-economy.ec.europa.eu/publications/annual-report-eu-smes_en;

Fair Trade Federation (FTF). 2025. About the Fair Trade Federation. Accessed May 14, 2025. https://www.fairtradefederation.org/about-ftf/.

Green Business Certification Inc. (GBCI). 2025. Certifications and Credentials. Accessed May 14, 2025. https://www.gbci.org/.

International Federation of Accountants (IFAC). 2023. The Importance of SMEs to the Global Economy. IFAC Official Website. Accessed May 14, 2025. https://www.ifac.org/knowledge-gateway/contributing-global-economy/discussion/importance-smes-global-economy.

KeepCup. 2025. Life Cycle Analysis Report. KeepCup Official Website. Accessed May 14, 2025. https://www.keepcup.com/en-au/life-cycle-analysis.

KeepCup. 2025. Our Mission and Environmental Impact. KeepCup Official Website. Accessed May 14, 2025. https://www.keepcup.com/en-au/our-mission.

King Arthur Baking Company. 2025. Our History and Values. King Arthur Baking Official Website. Accessed May 14, 2025. https://www.kingarthurbaking.com/about-us/our-history.

Little Yellow Bird. 2025. Our Story and Sustainability Commitment. Little Yellow Bird Official Website. Accessed May 14, 2025. https://www.littleyellowbird.com/pages/our-story.

McDonald's Corporation. 2024. Our Mission and Vision. McDonald's Official Website. Accessed May 13, 2025. https://corporate.mcdonalds.com/corpmcd/about-us/our-mission-and-values.html.

McKinsey Global Institute. 2022. Small Businesses: Driving Forces of Global Economic Growth. McKinsey & Company. Accessed May 13, 2025. https://www.mckinsey.com/featured-insights/small-businesses-driving-global-growth.

NORC at the University of Chicago. 2020. Assessing Progress in Reducing Child Labor in the Cocoa Sector of Côte devour and Ghana. U.S. Department of Labor. Accessed May 13, 2025. https://www.dol.gov/agencies/ilab/norc-child-labor-cocoa-study.

Organization for Economic Co-operation and Development (OECD). 2024. SMEs and Entrepreneurship: Key Statistics. OECD Official Website. Accessed May 13, 2025. https://www.oecd.org/industry/smes.

Pledge 1%. 2025. About Pledge 1%: Our Mission and Impact. Pledge 1% Official Website. Accessed May 13, 2025. https://pledge1percent.org/about/.

Regenerative Organic Alliance. 2024. ROC Certified Launches Canada's First Regenerative Organic Coffee. Regenerative Organic Alliance Newsroom. Accessed May 13, 2025. https://regenorganic.org/news.

Salt Spring Coffee. 2025. Our Story and Impact. Salt Spring Coffee Official Website. Accessed May 14, 2025. https://www.saltspringcoffee.com/pages/our-story.

Social Enterprise World Forum (SEWF). 2025. About SEWF. Accessed May 13, 2025. https://sewfonline.com/about/.

The Coca-Cola Company. 2024. Purpose and Mission. The Coca-Cola Company Official Website. Accessed May 13, 2025. https://www.coca-colacompany.com/company/purpose-and-mission.

Tony's Chocolonely. 2025. Our Mission and Impact. Tony's Chocolonely Official Website. Accessed May 13, 2025. https://tonyschocolonely.com/us/en/our-mission.

United Nations Department of Economic and Social Affairs. 2024. World Population Prospects 2024: Key Findings. United Nations. Accessed May 13, 2025. https://population.un.org/wpp/.

United Nations. 2023. Micro-, Small and Medium-Sized Enterprises Day Report. United Nations Official Website. Accessed May 14, 2025. https://www.un.org/en/observances/micro-small-medium-businesses-day.

U.S. Bureau of Labor Statistics. 2024. Business Employment Dynamics: Entrepreneurship and the Survival of New Businesses. U.S. Department of Labor. Accessed May 13, 2025. https://www.bls.gov/bdm/entrepreneurship/entrepreneurship.htm.

U.S. Census Bureau. 2024. Statistics of U.S. Businesses (SUSB). U.S. Department of Commerce. Accessed May 13, 2025. https://www.census.gov/programs-surveys/susb.html.

U.S. Internal Revenue Service (IRS). 2024. SOI Tax Stats - Sole Proprietorship Returns, 2022. Accessed May 13, 2025. https://www.irs.gov/statistics/soi-tax-stats-sole-proprietorship-returns.

U.S. Small Business Administration (SBA). 2024. 2024 Small Business Profile. U.S. SBA Office of Advocacy. Accessed May 13, 2025. https://advocacy.sba.gov.

U. S. Small Business Administration, Small Business Facts and Figures, 2024, accessed May 13, 2025, https://www.sba.gov.

World Bank Group. 2024. Small and Medium Enterprises (SMEs) Finance. The World Bank. Accessed May 13, 2025. https://www.worldbank.org/en/topic/smefinance.

PART TWO:
FINDING "THE EXTRA" TO SHARE

THIS IS THE TECHNICAL SECTION of how to build a stronger, longer lasting business that can help you find *your extra* to share and to be a good steward. If you prefer, you can read the entirety of this Part Two later and proceed to Part Three now to learn more about how your specific stewardship plan can be implemented. Another possibility is that you put your head down and get into the details about how to build a multi-generational small business–which changes everything. Instead of looking up and looking outward as in Parts One and Three, this Part Two is about looking down, sometimes with a magnifying glass in hand, and thinking through the details of your everyday business life.

A quick caveat. There are 195 countries in the world today. Each country has its own unique laws about how a small business should be set up, operated, regulated and taxed. The technical details in this Part Two are what I know and have worked with extensively and certainly mirror U.S. business and tax law. This book is written to and about small business owners around the world, but I must acknowledge my limitations and admit that I cannot adapt the technicalities to every jurisdiction around the world–at least not in one book! Please understand that the concepts in Part Two are what really matter. As my legal mentor told me once, long ago, "There's almost always a way…" if you look hard enough and know what you want to accomplish.

Moving forward, you should know going in that the entirety of Part Two focuses on your internal stakeholders:

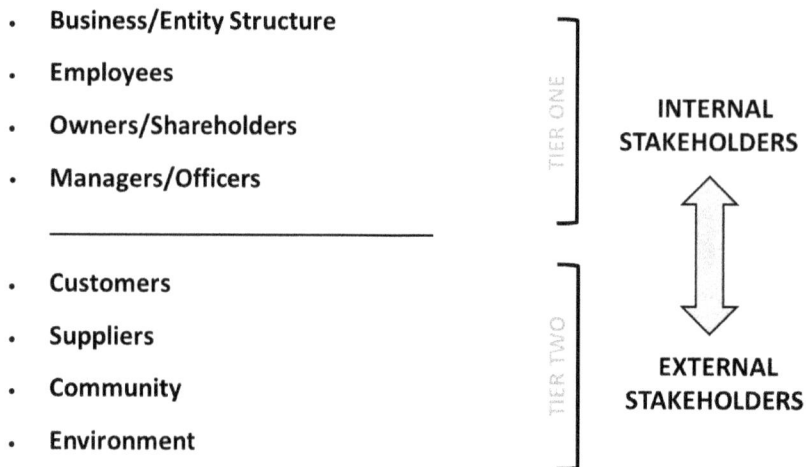

- **Business/Entity Structure**
- **Employees**
- **Owners/Shareholders**
- **Managers/Officers**

TIER ONE

INTERNAL STAKEHOLDERS

- **Customers**
- **Suppliers**
- **Community**
- **Environment**

TIER TWO

EXTERNAL STAKEHOLDERS

Figure 3

Through the separate sections in Part Two, you will learn the mechanics of the process of being **a good steward of equity**. Equity is about ownership and it is the difference maker if you want to build a business that outlives its founder(s). This is Tier One stuff. In the end, regardless of whether you decide to devote yourself to being a good steward for all of your stakeholders on a consistent and focused basis or just helping whenever and however you can while you earn a better living for your family, Part Two is designed to make you a better owner and leave you with a stronger business. Think of this as a direct assault on those high small business failure rates previously cited in Section 1.4.

Part Two is going to take some work. But if you were afraid of hard work, you wouldn't have started your own small business!

During the years I ran my own small businesses, I consulted with owners on how to strengthen and perpetuate their small businesses. In the process, I helped younger, next gen key employees buy into ownership. In order to create these multi-owner, multi-generational small businesses, the first tasks every time were to lay new, stronger foundations. The goal wasn't to build something larger and more complex, even if that sometimes happened. Many of these small businesses started out as sole proprietorships and ended up with ten to twenty owners and employees combined. The common goals were centered on building value, profitability, durability, and investability in a business geared for sustainable growth.

In the process of building these equity-centric businesses, next generation, first-time owners acquired and paid for a stake (i.e., a minority interest) in the same business that employed them. And I think that matters a lot. This is the path to durability and building a business that can last for generations, an integral part of the stewardship formula:

FOCUS + CONSISTENCY + **DURATION** = GOOD STEWARDSHIP

As buyers, these young professionals took out bank loans or relied on seller financing, and they willingly took the risk of ownership. Debt servicing could be as long as ten years per buy in. With multiple buy-ins, these opportunities often became a career length series of smaller investments. Motivation for these younger, first-time owners was rarely an issue. They needed to help grow their investment to generate the profits to pay for their equity–the value of which came to exceed virtually every other asset they owned.

In the last years of my work, I helped set up a hundred such multi-owner, multi-generational businesses every year, often with two or three next gen investors per small business. Nothing is perfect in this world or guaranteed as a small business owner, but our success rates were as close to it as possible. We will explore in the pages that follow exactly how to build such durability and investability into your small business. This is one of the keys to being a good steward of your internal stakeholders which, in turn, supports being a better steward to your external stakeholders.

The following sections of Part Two are essentially a condensed course on how to take your small business to a higher level so that you can do more with it and, hopefully, have more to share with the world around you. If you want or need more detail and you are already a small business owner, please consider reading my book *Building With the End in Mind*. If you are a next generation key employee, son or daughter, or ownership prospect, please read *Acquiring Your Future Through a Succession Plan*. This book series was recently published to give you the detail`s you need to get the job done. These books are all about building a multi-owner, multi-generational business that is more efficient and designed to last.

STEWARDSHIP SPOTLIGHT

soleREBELS (ADDIS ABABA, ETHIOPIA): This small business repurposes old tires by crafting them into the soles of their footwear—a modern interpretation of the traditional selate and bara basso shoes worn in Ethiopia for generations. It is all part of the company's mission to make the world a better place, one step at a time.

Founded in 2005, soleRebels employs between 100 to 150 workers (depending on production needs) and pays wages that are four times the legal minimum and three times the local industry average for similar work.

soleRebels was the first footwear company to be certified by the World Fair Trade Organization (WFTO), demonstrating a commitment to fair wages, safe working conditions, and ethical production practices. Recognizing that access to healthcare remains a challenge for many in Ethiopia, soleRebels provides medical insurance that covers employees and their families, helping to ease barriers to essential health services.

2.1 SETTING UP (OR ADJUSTING) A PROPER ENTITY STRUCTURE

You need an entity for your small business. Sole proprietorships and single owner businesses die with their owner, or sooner upon their owner's retirement, disability, or just calling it quits. An entity (e.g., corporation or LLC) can outlive its founding owner when properly built for the task.

Again, note that Part Two references U.S. based legal and tax structures. Also, depending on your entity of choice, you may be called an owner, a partner, a shareholder, a member, or even a principal–for the purposes of our exploration, it doesn't matter.

The basic entity choices we will explore are all tax conduits or flow-through structures, and that is for good reason. One of the terms that a good Tier One steward must become familiar with is that of *investability*. More precisely, why would a key employee, or even your son or daughter, *want to acquire an equity stake* in your small business? There are two keys to the answer. The first is profitability, especially in a tax conduit where profits usually flow home pro rata as a return on one's investment. The second reason is growth. As a business steadily grows over time, an owners' stock, or equity stake, can grow tax free (at least in the U.S.) until one day it is sold, and then usually at long-term capital gains rates. And for an active owner who comes in to work every day, which is the norm for a small business, that owner also receives separate compensation for the work that they do.

If you want to skip ahead to find the answer as to the best entity structure(s), I'll save you the trouble! The best entity structures for most small businesses are these:

- An LLC taxed as a DE/partnership

- An LLC taxed as an S corporation

- An S corporation

Why? Small businesses with approximately 100 or fewer owner/employees are different from larger businesses with thousands of owners and investors, public or private. In a small business, these flow-through structures support new owner/next generation investability. These structures also support flexibility and, in some cases, tax efficiency. Finally, these entity choices support "shareholder value" (covered in Section 2.6) which often makes small business ownership the single, largest, most valuable asset an entrepreneur owns. Each entity structure on this list is explained in greater detail below.

In contrast, you'll note that a C corporation is not on the short list for most small businesses. It is possible that your small business is the exception, so I will defer to qualified local tax counsel. But in my experience (thirty-plus years, former attorney and securities regulator, consulting in all fifty states and then some), this short list applies to 99 percent of small businesses in the U.S. And with that, let's explore what you need to know.

2.1.1 The Basics: Back in the day, I'd start my equity workshops by explaining that an entity structure is akin to the concrete footings put into place when building a new home. It is one of the very first steps in the building process, and arguably the most important. The concrete footings and stem walls, mostly below ground level, provide rigidity and load-bearing strength. Every part of the house is in one way or another attached to or supported by this solid foundation, built to last for generations. Generally, when the home is complete and ready for occupancy by the owner(s), these concrete support elements are mostly hidden from sight or barely noticed, but there is no house without this critical functional part of the whole. The same is true of the underlying entity structure in support of a durable business.

Additional benefits of setting up an appropriate entity, as opposed to a simpler sole proprietorship, include:

- Added formality and predictability as operations shift to a multi-owner, multi-generational business model

- A clear separation of the business's assets, liabilities, and cash flows from that of the owner(s)

- A clear and effective governance structure supported by officers, directors, shareholders, and employees

- Limited liability for the equity owners in certain situations

- Potential tax savings or tax efficiencies

You should anticipate that your *initial entity of choice* will be your forever choice. It is sometimes possible to change the entity and/or its underlying tax structure in the years to come, as I'll explain below, but it is usually not easy, common, or inexpensive. The key is to build adequate flexibility into your initial choice if you can foresee your needs far enough in advance—another good reason to know your purpose as a business. If you have already set up your entity and are feeling less certain about it, one possible adjustment period may emerge in Section 2.2 below that allows you to make one last, permanent changeover.

Legally separating your personal income and assets from those of your business is another major benefit of having an entity structure. This is not just practical, it is a benefit often associated with limited liability—not an absolute blanket of coverage, but an attribute better had than not. To make a small business valuable and investable, it must operate and exist separately from its owners' personal finances and assets. An entity helps to create a clear line of demarcation between individuals and the business they own and/or have invested in.

Some entities such as C corporations and LLCs taxed as partnerships can issue more than one class of stock, but in most cases, a small business with fewer than 100 employees only needs one class of equity. A second class may be needed at some point in the future, but often not until the business value is $20.0 million or more. In that single class, an entity can generally authorize and issue as many shares of stock as it wishes. As a general rule, however, I'd start on the high side (100,000 shares minimum or, preferably, 1,000,000 shares—but not 10 or 100 shares, which would need to be adjusted later on). Authorizing a larger number of shares initially provides flexibility for future growth, employee incentives, potential mergers, tax-neutral exchanges, and acquisitions. The simple goal is to keep your price per share down to single or double digits for maximum flexibility and ease of operation.

Not sure where to start? Think big! If you're wrong, you have nothing to lose. If you're right, you will need strong, durable, flexible, efficient foundations to build your small business on. Talk to your local legal and/or tax counsel about your needs and goals.

2.1.2 How an LLC Works: The use of a limited liability company, or LLC, is an increasingly prevalent choice among small business owners because it is an exceptionally flexible and fluid structure. In effect, an LLC can change its underlying tax election, or status, from that of a sole proprietorship to a partnership, to a C corporation, to an S corporation over time. An LLC is the only entity that can do so to this extent. For this reason, if a choice exists as to an entity and you or the founders are not absolutely sure of the best course of action, an LLC is the place to start. It can be what you need it to be and it can adapt over time as your business evolves.

"When we strive to become better than we are, everything around us becomes better too."

Paulo Coelho
(Brazil)

Under the LLC format, once filed, the founding owner or owners can choose, as a group, to have the LLC taxed in one of the following four ways:

1) a DE, or disregarded entity (if there is only one owner)

2) a partnership (if there are two or more owners)

3) a C corporation, or

4) an S corporation

This is indeed a very flexible structure, perhaps more so than might first appear. This tax election process (the ability to choose how you want your LLC to be taxed), along with the ability to subsequently change the election under certain circumstances as your business needs change, is why an LLC is often the preferred initial choice. With a single filing, your LLC can be whatever the ownership group needs it to be within the bounds of the law and tax code. As a result, there is almost no good reason not to set up an LLC as the basic or initial structure. The nomenclature used in this book to refer to an LLC that elects to be taxed as a DE, partnership, or S corporation, is simply LLC/DE, LLC/partnership, or LLC/S corporation, respectively.

The election of tax treatment is made solely with the IRS, and then each state in which the business operates will recognize the entity as such. If there is just one owner of an LLC, it is automatically taxed as a DE unless it files an S corporation election (Form 2553). If there are two or more owners of an LLC, it is automatically taxed as a partnership unless it files a Form 2553. An LLC with two or more owners may file a Form 8832 with the IRS to declare that it intends to be taxed as a partnership, but it does not have to. Technically, the IRS does not recognize an LLC for tax purposes—it is the underlying election that matters to the taxing authorities.

As an additional benefit, an LLC affords its equity owners, acting together, the ability to *migrate* between these four choices. The most practical way to think about it is that one can migrate from the first choice (DE) to the fourth choice (S corporation) *as a one-way trip*. If you migrate over time from an LLC/DE with one owner to an LLC/partnership with two or more owners, and then to an LLC/C corporation that makes an S corporation election, you will probably need to retain your S corporation tax status from then on as there can be significant taxes/penalties to backtrack after the business has grown substantially. There are a lot of rules and exceptions to additionally consider, but these are the important basics of an LLC to be aware of.

Starting on the ground floor with the first choice, an LLC treated by the tax authorities as a DE is a one-owner entity structure. In fact, the IRS treats the owner as a sole proprietorship, albeit one with limited liability in some instances. Initially, and often until next generation owners join the business, many LLCs start out as a DE. Once there is a second owner, the tax election defaults from a DE to that of a partnership, although the addition of a new owner is the time to make a purposeful election of your preferred tax classification, which at this writing is accomplished by filing Internal Revenue Service form 8832.

An LLC taxed as a partnership is a unique entity choice affording the widest range of flexibility to a growing, changing business, especially over several generations and perhaps in a regulated profession (if that includes you). For example, an LLC/partnership can accommodate multiple classes of equity should the ownership team ever need that option. Partnership law also allows owners to allocate profits and losses based upon criteria other than their ownership percentage, and it may eliminate or reduce state-mandated record-keeping requirements imposed on corporations, such as annual meetings and minutes.

An LLC/partnership offers a distinct advantage over all the other entity structuring options in that it allows for the exchange of an incoming owner's book (cash flow, client relationships, goodwill) of clients, if they have one, for equity in the LLC/partnership in a tax-neutral manner. This permits the business to "onboard" or merge in next generation talent. This is a powerful growth and talent acquisition/retention tool under the right circumstances. Onboarding talent is technically called a tax-neutral exchange (Internal Revenue Code §721) and can quickly reset the table of a small business equity structure.

It is not all good news when using an LLC/partnership structure. There are a couple of issues to be aware of. An LLC/partnership, unlike an LLC/S corporation or even a basic S corporation, cannot treat an owner as a W2 employee (covered in Section 2.1.3), and it cannot offer tax savings on the payment of profit distribution dollars as is commonplace for an S corporation or LLC/S corporation in many states. As a former owner of an LLC/partnership, I can also attest that this is a fairly sophisticated entity structure. What that means is that you may need an experienced accountant or CPA who has experience providing guidance to other small businesses with the same entity and tax structure you have chosen. And sometimes it means that you will need a tax attorney to resolve or take advantage of an LLC/partnership issue or opportunity.

2.1.3 How an S Corporation Works: A basic S corporation (i.e., not an LLC making an S corporation election) can be a smart choice for many small businesses that want to be a good steward of equity. Most small business owners, as well as their attorneys and accountants, consider an S corporation to be the simplest entity structure (technically a corporation is an entity and an S corporation is a tax election) to understand and operate—a real benefit if you'd rather work *in your business* than on it. An S corporation, basic or under an LLC, offers these important benefits in most states:

- Shareholders can receive treatment as W2 employees of the business

- A shareholder receives a pro rata share of profits/losses and stock appreciation as a matter of law

- S corporations escape the double taxation of a C corporation and, in most states, profits flow through to owners at a lower tax rate than wages (i.e., the self-employment tax savings)

- Limited liability in certain respects

- Unlimited life—for an S corporation with multiple owners, it will continue to exist after the death, withdrawal, or departure of any one of the owners

- A tax-conduit or flow-through structure

An S corporation must meet and maintain certain requirements throughout the entire tax year, typically the calendar year, in order to qualify for these unique benefits. Among these requirements are that the entity must be either a U.S. formed LLC or corporation, it cannot have more than 100 shareholders, it is limited to just one class of stock, and it must distribute profits and losses pro rata to ownership. Additionally, all shareholders must be natural persons or qualified trusts and U.S. citizens or legal residents of the U.S., residing in the U.S. If, for example, one of four shareholders who is a U.S. citizen becomes a resident of a foreign country, the subchapter S election could terminate, potentially affecting *all* the shareholders and their tax obligations.

One of the most important benefits of an S corporation or an LLC/S corporation can be the self-employment tax savings (Social Security and Medicare). It is possible, with guidance from your tax advisor, to reasonably divide the business proceeds after expenses are paid into FICA (Federal Insurance Contributions Act)-taxable wages (subject to the many federal, state, and local taxes tied to employment compensation, and which may also include assessments for unemployment and workers compensation) and FICA-exempt profit distributions. In sum, an S corporation only pays wage-based taxes on compensation to its owners and not on the remaining profits paid out as distributions. We will explore how to purposefully and professionally isolate these profit distributions in Section 2.4.

An S corporation must pay *a reasonable salary* to a shareholder who may also be a W-2 employee. The profits that remain after deducting reasonable compensation and operating expenses is not subject to the federal self-employment tax. Note that city, county, and state taxes can significantly affect the choice and use of an S corporation and erode any tax savings, and this is an ever-changing landscape. Guidance on this front should come from your local tax advisor before setting up or making an S corporation election.

Reasonable compensation is the wage or salary that is paid to a business owner to perform services for the business before receiving a profit distribution in an S corporation or an LLC/S corporation. In the simplest of terms, to be considered "reasonable" by the IRS (always in hindsight), the amount paid must be equivalent to what a similar business would pay someone else with similar qualifications and experience to perform the same or similar services. The IRS looks at many factors to determine if you or another owner met this requirement if you're audited on this issue.

In sum, there are many good reasons to organize your small business using an S corporation or an LLC/S corporation entity structure, or even to be a next gen owner of such an entity. Younger owners of a minority interest often appreciate the pro rata requirements and any tax savings on their share of the profits and appreciating stock value.

There are a couple of drawbacks to be aware of when using an S corporation tax structure. First, once the founders have set up an entity and elect S corporation taxation and then contribute in their capital assets (a process covered in Section 2.2), the entity will have an ascertainable and, perhaps, significant value; if not now, then in the future. Changing from an S corporation to an entity taxed as anything else (LLC/partnership or LLC/DE or even a sole proprietorship) can come with a tax bill on what the tax authorities often consider a liquidation event for the S corporation. Second, S corporations cannot easily or inexpensively onboard or merge in next generation talent with a book of clients via a tax-neutral exchange, the unique territory of an LLC/partnership. Third, all of an S corporation's shareholders must agree to strictly abide by federal restrictions to retain the benefits of an S corporation election; carelessness or an oversight by any one shareholder can result in retroactive treatment as a C corporation with double taxation, which can be expensive. Finally, to enjoy any tax savings, you have to run a payroll. Though I would consider this a normal and natural part of a growing business and a necessary part of being a good Tier One steward, payrolls usually require a bookkeeper, an accountant, and meticulous record keeping.

STEWARDSHIP SPOTLIGHT

PROVINCE APOTHECARY (TORONTO, ONTARIO, CANADA): Province Apothecary (PA) is a skincare and wellness brand recognized for its strong commitment to organic, natural, and sustainable practices. PA prides itself on sourcing the highest quality certified organic and wildcrafted ingredients from across Canada—supporting local biodiversity and ensuring the potency of its formulations. The brand is cruelty-free, and many of its products are certified vegan, aligning with ethical and sustainable consumer values.

As founder Julie Clark explains:

"When I started PA, we gave back to the Canadian Organic Growers and Canadian Honey Council because it was so difficult to find organic raw ingredients in Canada, and we were hoping to make a positive impact on their growth and accessibility. As the brand evolved, our focus has shifted to supporting our community and people, as well as the environment."

Giving back is at the heart of Province Apothecary's ethos. Every year, the company donates a percentage of its sales to several organizations, including its partnership with 1% for the Planet.

2.2 SHIFTING VALUE TO YOUR ENTITY

Establishing the proper entity or amending your current structure to support a growing, valuable, profitable and investable business is the first step in creating an enduring foundation. The second step, addressed in this section, is literally and legally transferring the assets of the individual founder(s) or owner(s) into the entity. This is how you convert personally owned and controlled assets into equity which can become profitable, valuable, investable, and durable. And it is a major part of separating personal assets from business assets.

From this point on, I will refer to your new entity, or your rebuilt entity, as "Newco."

Pause for a moment, please, and focus on this and the next couple of paragraphs. Small business owners, and even their legal and tax counsel, often overlook this step, but your next generation investors won't. This is the step that makes your business both valuable and investable. This is what you need to know: the assets of a sole proprietorship or individual owner are basically these, regardless of the profession one is engaged in:

a) The clients (or client list) being served

b) The annualized cash flow generated from serving the clients

c) Any tangible property (the physical tools of the trade or profession, whatever they may be), and

d) Goodwill

On occasion, one might add "Intellectual Property" to this list (i.e., inventions, creative works, designs, brand names, copyrights or trademarks, and logos). Collectively, these are your capital assets.

A valuable and investable business starts with a transfer of these capital assets from an individual owner(s) into Newco. Newco then issues equity as shares of stock or units (as they're often called in an LLC) to each contributing owner. If there is one owner who previously operated as a sole proprietorship and now operates Newco as an S corporation, then this one owner will hold all the 100,000 issued shares of stock in exchange, for example; if there are two founding owners, they might each hold 50,000 shares of stock in Newco, or their pro rata share.

As a result of this formal exchange process, Newco then becomes the legal owner of those valuable capital assets, including all future clients and related revenue. The contributor or founding owner(s) becomes a shareholder of Newco. All of this typically happens privately, quietly, and without any kind of government oversight (state or federal, at least in the U.S.) when setting up a new entity like Newco. At this stage of the initial process, the transformation from a sole proprietorship or an individual to a business formally occurs. If you've already set up a different type of entity but have not made a contribution of capital assets into the entity, there is a good argument that the entity has no value and could be terminated in favor of a better choice with limited tax repercussions. These are decisions to be made after discussion with local legal and tax counsel, of course.

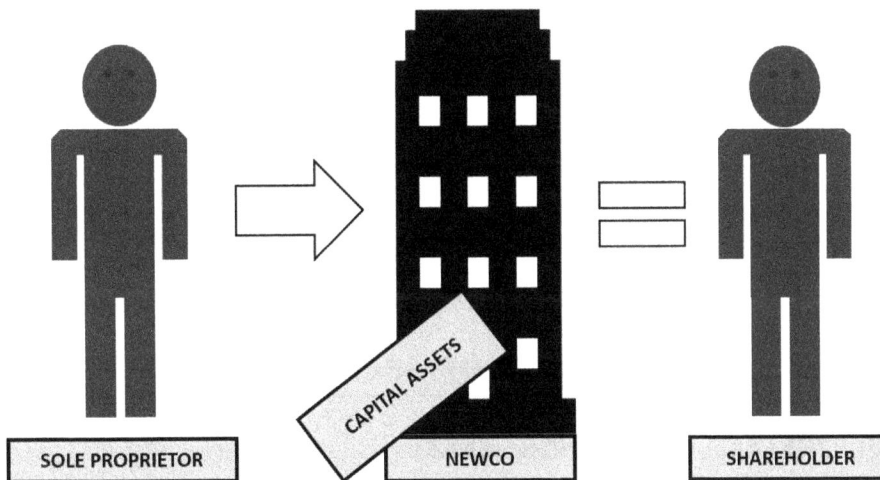

Figure 4

More simply, consider Newco's decision to be taxed as an S corporation upon setup with 100,000 authorized voting shares in a single class. The lone contributing and founding owner in this example, Becka, moves from individual or sole proprietor to shareholder with her conveyance of all of her capital assets to Newco. Now, Becka owns 100,000 authorized and issued shares of voting stock, *and Newco owns all the capital assets.*

Here is why this matters. An appraiser can now value the capital assets that Newco legally holds and effectively determine a price per share. In other words, the business now has an ascertainable value. If the business is valued at $1,250,000, for example, then each share of stock that Becka owns is objectively worth $12.50/share. Becka is then able to sell some of these shares to her key employee, Zach, who can choose to invest in these appraised shares and, if necessary, obtain a bank loan to support his equity purchase. And, once Zach is fully invested, retaining his talents and motivating him to help grow the business changes significantly for the better. This is building for long-term success, and we're just getting started.

It is also possible that one or more individuals (think sole proprietorships) could simultaneously make such contributions into Newco upon its setup, effectively resulting in a merger of those individual client books via a series of tax-neutral exchanges. Newco might begin operations with two, three, or four partners at one time, a process I've consulted on many times. In such a case, Newco now owns ALL the contributed capital assets with each contributor owning equity, or stock, proportionally. In most cases, this exchange process can be accomplished with no cash payments or any immediate tax consequences to the participants if the rules are followed carefully and completely (under the Internal Revenue Code, or IRC). This is a common method of forming a new business with multiple contributing new owners and tends to rely on use of an LLC/partnership.

Of course, as television shows used to say, "Don't try this at home!" These strategies and maneuvers require professional assistance. You just need to know enough to ask the right questions.

STEWARDSHIP SPOTLIGHT

LAUDE THE LABEL (FORT WORTH, TEXAS): LAUDE the Label was founded in 2014 by Carly Burson, driven by a desire to leverage her experience in the fashion industry as a platform to meaningfully employ and empower women around the world. Her mission—to help preserve families through living wages, educational training, safe work environments, and access to the global marketplace—has helped advance larger conversations around sustainability and ethical practices within the fashion industry.

This small business is a verified member of the Fair Trade Federation and ensures that artisans are paid above standard fair trade wage requirements. LAUDE the Label emphasizes safe working conditions and equal opportunities for advancement, while prioritizing the use of organic, earth-friendly natural fibers such as organic cotton and linen, along with upcycled and recycled materials to minimize environmental impact. For each package shipped, the company invests in the planting and monitoring of a tree. Although previously certified as a B Corporation, LAUDE the Label voluntarily chose to step away from third-party certification to focus directly on its community-driven mission.

2.3 UNDERSTANDING HOW STOCK/EQUITY IS BOUGHT AND SOLD

THIS SECTION IS ALL ABOUT small businesses becoming good stewards of equity, or ownership, on behalf of their internal stakeholders.

My advice to every founding owner that I've consulted with over the past thirty years has been simple and consistent on one key point. Stock, or any form of equity, in a valuable and growing business should never be treated like a birthday present. It should not be given away or granted; although discounted and financed are different issues and often provide some remediation.

This is not meant to dash the hopes and dreams of the next gen ownership prospects, sons or daughters, out there who feel underpaid and entitled to some equity as a result. The truth is that closely held, restricted, and regulated stock has as many continuing obligations as it does opportunities. And owners of equity in the context of a small business are usually actively involved in the long-term success and growth of the business they buy into. This requires an investment mindset on the part of the buyer/employee.

"A word after a word after a word is power."

Margaret Atwood
(Canada)

In any given equity transaction between an existing owner, often the business's founder or founders, and a next generation prospective owner, there are actually three or more participants involved when viewed through the lens of a small business:

- The individual seller(s)

- The individual buyer

- The entity, or Newco

Depending on whether the selling owner finances the transaction, or a bank or credit union is used, there may be a fourth participant.

The entity participant, Newco, presents numerous intriguing options and alternatives that every business owner should have at least a passing familiarity with. In the process of becoming a good Tier One steward, the basic rule is that *individuals* buy equity and *individuals* sell equity. In fact, this is how most transactions in a small business occur. To be clear, equity in this context refers to shares of stock that one owns in a business, or Newco in this case.

But Newco, as an entity, will also have its own shares of stock, properly termed as *authorized but unissued shares*. Effectively, these shares are *sitting on a shelf* somewhere at the business and don't count until and unless they are actually issued. It is very common to have such extra shares made available upon the entity's setup.

It is technically and legally possible to have a new owner buy stock directly from Newco rather than an individual owner. It is also possible that an existing owner could sell some of their shares back to Newco, but these possibilities are the exceptions rather than the rules and exceed our purposes of learning to be good equity stewards. I wrote a series of books on such intricacies if you're interested, and the titles are listed in the front of this book or under my authorship on most book distribution sites.

Staying on course and to better explain the details of these individual-to-individual stock transactions, let's reset the table and get specific. At the time Newco is filed and initially set up, or reorganized if you already have an entity, the supporting documentation should include some adjustments, or additions, to the typical entity to accommodate the strategies involved in this long-term thinking:

1. Authorize 200,000 shares of voting stock

2. Issue 100,000 shares of that voting stock to the founders and any other immediate owners in exchange for their contributions of capital assets and/or cash

3. Elect tax treatment as an LLC/S corporation or, if a tax-neutral exchange strategy is relevant, an LLC/partnership

To clarify, 200,000 shares are authorized, and half of that—100,000 shares—are issued, leaving 100,000 shares authorized but unissued, *and sitting on the shelf*. These terms (issued and unissued) can really matter over time in a growing multi-owner/multi-generational business, but it helps to plan ahead (or declare a stock dividend when the time comes!).

In an initial sale of stock, or equity, let's say we have two owners, "A" and "B" who are the founders of Newco. These two individuals own 80 percent and 20 percent of the stock of Newco after their capital contributions respectively ("A" owns 80,000 shares and "B" owns 20,000 shares, with 100,000 additional shares authorized but unissued). "A" agrees to sell 10,000 shares of stock to new owner "C," and 10,000 shares to younger partner "B," both of whom obtain conventional bank loans and acquire the shares at fair market value (FMV) as determined by an appraiser. (Every purchase or sale of small business stock should be preceded by a professional appraisal and full and complete due diligence on the part of the buyer/investor.)

Owner "B" is now a 30 percent owner, and owner "C" will be a 10 percent owner, provided they both continue to make all payments on time and in full. These investments should also serve to motivate both owners and any other next generation owners that follow to grow the business while carefully watching overhead and focusing on the bottom line, which is how they will service the debt, acquire more equity, and build their own wealth. Profits matter to a multi-generational business, and that can be a very good thing for all the stakeholders.

Profits are what power the engine that runs a small business, especially one that is considered investable. Profits are a major reason why the next generation buys in. It is how the next generation pays for the opportunity. It is what makes a small business valuable to the founders and how they recoup their significant risk and investment even as they gradually pass the baton to the second generation of leadership.

In most cases, wages and benefits are not enough to attract and retain active investor-level talent to help you build and grow a multi-generational business. Well managed profitability is the way to be a good steward of your internal stakeholders for generations to come. That is what we will delve into in the following section.

STEWARDSHIP SPOTLIGHT

INTEGRATED WEALTH PLANNING (LEXINGTON, KENTUCKY): As good stewards, Jeffrey Todd and Brandon Gaines operate a multi-owner, multi-generational small business built for long-term success. These gentlemen have implemented many of the business strengthening strategies outlined in Part Two of this book.

At Integrated Wealth Planning (IWP), stewardship is fully integrated into the daily business operations. IWP contributes to organizations such as St. Jude Children's Research Hospital, Alex's Lemonade Stand, Charity:Water, Folds of Honor, and the ALS Association. Their annual stewardship contributions are matched up to $10,000 by Northwestern Mutual Life Insurance (NM), their parent company; a major benefit that extends beyond the generosity of IWP.

Across the United States, more than 7,000 financial advisors and professionals affiliated with NM–operating as independent small businesses—enjoy this corporate support as they serve over five million clients. This kind of partnership between small and large businesses offers a compelling model for expanding stewardship impact on a local and national scale.

2.4 RETHINKING YOUR BUSINESS'S CASH FLOWS

MANY SMALL BUSINESS OWNERS MANAGE cash flow by paying expenses first, then keeping what's left over for themselves. I often refer to this as a two-basket cash flow system since everything flows one place or the other. In this model, high revenue often feels like high profitability. But in this section, we'll rethink that approach. You'll learn a simple but powerful system for running your business like a business—not like your personal piggy bank (respectfully). I have helped thousands of small business owners learn this powerful cash flow management technique which, in turn, supports a number of other important strategies to help you run a more profitable, valuable and durable business.

Once Newco is properly set up, a business bank account can be opened. From this moment onward, with all capital assets having been properly and legally transferred into Newco (your new or rebuilt entity), all incoming revenue generated by and through Newco will be deposited into the business's primary checking account. That revenue now belongs to Newco of which you are an owner or shareholder. This revenue becomes the top line of Newco's profit and loss statement (P&L), forming the starting point for understanding profitability.

This income should then be *compartmentalized* as it flows through the P&L to more clearly illustrate a number of important concepts. Picture all business revenue flowing into one of three baskets:

- **Basket No. 1**: General operating expenses (everything needed to keep the business running, except owner wages)

- **Basket No. 2**: Owner wages or base salaries (compensation for the work owners actively perform)

- **Basket No. 3**: Profits—what remains after Basket Nos. 1 and 2 are fully funded.

GROSS REVENUE ($$$)

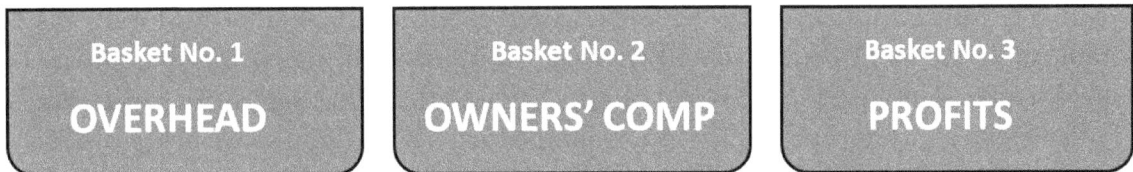

Basket No. 1	Basket No. 2	Basket No. 3
OVERHEAD	**OWNERS' COMP**	**PROFITS**

Figure 5

The goal of this Three-Basket Cash Flow System is to protect the financial health of your business, separate your wages from your profits, and maximize profitability for growth, reinvestment, and ownership rewards. To this end, Basket Nos. 1 and 2 serve to acknowledge that everyone, including and especially the owner(s), must be paid for the work that they do. But these two baskets also provide notice that not every dollar of revenue after overhead expenses from Basket No. 1 have been paid is allocated to the owner's salary as it would be in a sole proprietorship, the common training grounds for most entrepreneurs.

"What makes the desert beautiful is that somewhere it hides a well."

Antoine de Saint-Exupéry
(France)

In fact, there may be tax advantages to be gained by isolating and limiting the amount of money (within reason) paid through Basket No. 2 in deference to Basket No. 3—depending on your location, tax code, and entity structuring options. In the end, it is Basket No. 3, profits or profitability (technically, your net profit margin (NPM) as explained below in this section), which is the measure of success and the primary determinant of business value. To an investor, a term used broadly to include all owners of the business, Basket No. 3 provides the return on each owners' investment, or ROI. Every small business and venue and country is unique, but let's start out with a guideline of 25 percent profitability as a reasonable, near-term future goal and adjust from there, acknowledging that some small businesses can only generate half that, and others, twice that. This strategy and logic still apply even if *normal* profitability for your business is much lower.

This is not "the envelope method" of cash management–managing a small business's cash flow, growth, and tax rates is more complicated than that–sophisticated might be the better word. Profits (Basket No. 3) and equity appreciation (rising business value) together create long-term wealth for owners and key team members. Basket No. 3 is telling because, as profit levels increase, it supports higher business value (and therefore stock price). In addition, and coupled with strong top-line growth, profits may flow home at a lower tax rate, attract talent that aspires to ownership, and helps to pay for any equity being purchased, all the results of being a good steward of equity (Tier One). This is how you can change your corner of the world and find that extra to share or contribute. Being a good steward does not come at the cost of your net profit margin; at least in a small business, it is *because of* your net profit margin. This isn't the full and complete answer, mind you, but it is the start of something better.

If Newco, for example, generates $1,000,000/year in gross revenue for services rendered, then after Basket Nos. 1 and 2 are satisfied, $250,000 flows into the remaining basket as profitability. In most cases, profits flow to each owner, pro rata. The only way to access the dollars in Basket No. 3, however, is to take the risk of ownership and acquire an equity interest (for cash, a bank note, or by contributing one's capital assets). Increasing the amount and percentage of dollars flowing through Basket No. 3 is what makes a small business valuable and investable. In this example, understand that 25% profitability is not automatic or achieved immediately by cutting the dollars from the first two baskets. It usually takes time, growth and a plan.

For those small business owners whose venue requires much higher overhead (Basket No. 1) that, in turn, reduces profitability to the 10 percent to 15 percent range, please keep reading. The lessons on how to balance cash flows more effectively and how to use equity to hold expenses and salaries down in favor of more tax efficient rewards (stock appreciation and profit distributions) are still very much worth considering. At the very least, bolstering your profitability by even a couple of percentage points over your competitors could change the value of your business significantly.

This Three-Basket Cash Flow System sets the stage for a deeper look at your profitability measures—gross profit margin, operating profit margin, and net profit margin—each of which shows how efficiently your revenue flows through each basket on the path to true business profitability, or NPM. Of course, anything and everything works in this system when there is just one owner; modeling for two or three owners is a revelation which we will also explore further.

2.4.1. Understanding the Terminology. As you consider how to best use your small business to help change the world, it is important to understand the various profitability terms so that you mean the same thing as your accountant or bookkeeper or team leaders. Many stewardship ideas and goals include donating a percentage of revenue or profits to a worthy cause of your choice–but this is where the details matter. We'll begin with your **Gross Profit Margin** (or GPM), which tells you how much you're making from your core service(s) *before* considering your general business expenses.

Assume you delivered core goods or services for $1,000. This is how to calculate your gross profit margin:

- Gross Profit = Revenue (Sales) - Cost of Goods Sold (COGS) and/or Cost of Services (COS)

- Gross Profit Margin = (Gross Profit / Revenue) x 100 percent

In our continuing example, let's do the math:

- The *direct costs* associated with producing your core goods or delivering your core services were $200. These are your COGS and/or COS.

- Gross Profit = $1,000 (Revenue) - $200 (COGS or COS) = $800

- Gross Profit Margin = ($800 / $1,000) x 100 percent = 80 percent

To clarify a potential point of confusion, general operating expenses (OPEX) are NOT subtracted when calculating GPM. OPEX includes things like rent, utilities, office supplies, administrative staff wages and benefits, marketing and sales, technology and software, insurance, depreciation and amortization—items addressed in the next part of this terminology lesson. For a professional services business, the primary COS is usually direct, client-facing labor but can also include other client-facing personnel involved *in actually delivering the services.*

Why does GPM matter to you as a small business owner? This 80 percent result means that for every $1 you earn from your core goods or services, you have $0.80 left over to cover all your other operating expenses since your direct, client-facing costs have already been accounted for in the GPM calculation. Your gross profit margin shows how efficient you are, or aren't, at delivering your core goods or services and managing the direct costs. Tracking your gross profit margin over several years is very informative, especially when trying to diagnose a particular business shortcoming or when forecasting the cost of a new opportunity such as stewardship.

Next, we'll address your **Operating Profit Margin** (or OPM), which shows your profitability after you've accounted for the general operating expenses (OPEX) of running your small business but *before* considering interest, taxes, and other nonoperating items. Assume you delivered core goods or services for $1,000. This is how to calculate your OPM:

- Operating Profit = Gross Profit - Operating Expenses

- Operating Profit Margin = (Operating Profit / Revenue) x 100 percent

In our continuing example, let's say that your general operating expenses for the period are $450:

- Operating Profit = $800 (Gross Profit) - $450 (Operating Expenses) = $350

- Operating Profit Margin = ($350 / $1,000) x 100 percent = 35 percent

Why does OPM matter to you? This 35 percent result indicates how profitable your core operations are, or aren't, after covering your normal, routine operating costs. OPM tells you, as an owner, how well you are managing overhead and operating structure, not just delivery efficiency. It is a good indicator of how well you're managing your overall business.

As you work through the differences between your GPM and your OPM, it might help you to think of it like this:

1. **Revenue** (all the money you bring in from clients and/or goods you've sold)

2. **Minus direct costs**

3. **Equals gross profit**

4. **Minus general operating expenses**

5. Equals Operating Profit

Your OPM provides a broader view of profitability than GPM by taking into account *all* the costs of running your small business beyond just the direct cost of delivering services. An accountant or bookkeeper can help you work through these calculations and distinguish between different expense categories. And, again, remember that tracking these results is most useful over time as you see your business grow and evolve.

Finally, let's consider **Net Profit Margin** (or NPM)**.** This is your "bottom line" profit margin, or Basket No. 3 in our cash flow management system. It shows your profitability after *all* expenses have been deducted. Note that for most small businesses, net profit reflects the final profitability of the business itself before considering any personal income taxes that the owner(s) may owe. Since most small businesses operate as pass-through entities when possible, *personal taxes* are addressed separately and are not deducted on the business's profit and loss statement.

Again, assume you delivered core goods or services for $1,000. This is how to calculate your NPM:

- Net Profit Margin = (Net Profit / Revenue) x 100 percent

In our continuing example, let's assume you had $50 in interest expenses for a loan or line of credit and another $50 in miscellaneous, onetime expenses.

- Net Profit = $350 (Operating Profit) - $50 (Interest) - $50 (Misc) = $250

- Net Profit Margin = ($250 / $1,000) x 100 percent = 25 percent

Why does NPM matter to you? This 25 percent result is your final profit margin for your business's core operations during the period. It is the percentage of your revenue that actually ends up as profit after all costs and obligations are met. This is the money you ultimately get to take home (or reinvest in your business). As an owner and investor, this is our ROI.

By tracking these distinct profit margins—gross, operating, and net—you gain a much clearer picture of your business's financial health. This insight allows you to evaluate pricing decisions, operating efficiency, and long-term sustainability with far greater precision. The Three-Basket Cash Flow System gives structure to that process by aligning your day-to-day cash management with your profit margins, helping you rebuild your cash flow system from the bottom line up. Finding your extra starts with strengthening and increasing your net profit margin. Think of this first section in Part Two as assembling the essential tools in your business building toolbox. In the next section, we'll begin using profitability as a guidepost—not just for measuring success, but for shaping smarter, more durable decisions across your entire business.

STEWARDSHIP SPOTLIGHT

THE HAPPY PEAR (WICKLOW, IRELAND): The Happy Pear began in 2004 with the mission of creating a healthier, happier world and building community. Founded by twin brothers Stephen and David Flynn in Greystones, County Wicklow, Ireland, The Happy Pear is known for its focus on healthy, plant-based food and its vibrant, community-oriented approach.

Through their cafés, cookbooks, online courses, and dynamic social media presence, this small business actively educates and inspires people worldwide to incorporate more fruits, vegetables, and plant-based meals into their diets—supporting both personal health and a more sustainable food system.

Today, The Happy Pear operates its original veg shop, a café and bakery in Greystones, a four-acre regenerative organic farm, and a coffee roastery. They offer over 80 plant-based food products (with 15 million units sold), fifteen-plus online courses (completed by more than 100,000 participants), a recipe club, and seven cookbooks that have sold over 500,000 copies. Their social media following has grown to nearly 2 million people.

And for a cheerful break, their YouTube series—such as Walking in Wicklow with The Happy Pear—captures the same spirit of joy, health, and community that drives their business every day.

2.5 USING PROFITABILITY AS YOUR GUIDEPOST

IN BUILDING A SMALL BUSINESS for long-term success as well as enhancing stewardship efforts, profitability is the key. Ironically, I'd argue that every expense item, including wages for your staff members and support team, must be run through the filter of your profitability goal. This isn't to say that you should cut your expenses to increase your profit margins—that makes no sense in a small business built, or building, for long-term success. But you do have to live within your budgetary means as your business grows; half of your stakeholders are internal to your business.

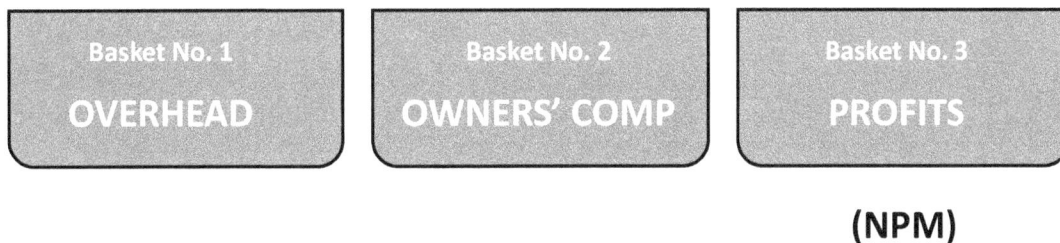

Basket No. 1	Basket No. 2	Basket No. 3
OVERHEAD	**OWNERS' COMP**	**PROFITS**

(NPM)

Figure 6

In the preceding section, you read this: *If Newco, for example, generates $1,000,000/ year in gross revenue for services rendered, then after Basket Nos. 1 and 2 are satisfied, $250,000 flows into the remaining basket as profitability.* Let's build on this concept of 25 percent profitability (i.e., net profit margin) and explore this at a higher level.

In the first few years of operation, or as you begin to rethink your cash flow management strategy, you might find that your three cash flow baskets are around 60%/20%/20%, (overhead / owners' comp / net profits). We will call these your "performance ratios." Over time, as your business matures and you gain experience and work toward building a more valuable, profitable, investable, and durable business, your performance ratios should improve with revenue growth to something in the percentage range of 50/25/25 to 40/30/30 (overhead / owners' comp / profits).

A longer term cash flow model of 35/30/35 or even 30/30/40 changes everything from an investor's point of view, depending, of course, on your professional services venue and normal, competitive overhead levels for a small business in your area.

Initially, as a small business owner in the first few years, figure out your overhead (Basket No. 1), your minimum take-home pay (Basket No. 2), and then what's left (Basket No. 3/NPM), if anything. As your business evolves, and sooner than later in any event, it is important and necessary to learn to run your business from the other direction. Start from your minimal, acceptable level of profitability (or NPM) and work backwards. Do this with input from your accountant, bookkeeper, and benchmarking data from similar businesses if available. You cannot reasonably pay yourself as the owner, or owners, a zero salary or even anything significantly below market indefinitely and retain talent and attract next gen investment to perpetuate your business. Still, forecast a reasonable salary at some point in the near future and do the math. What do you have available to run your business in terms of general expenses or overhead? This is where you'll learn to run your small business like a big business.

If the math doesn't work, it isn't a reason to stomp on the brakes; it is a guidepost to help you adjust course. Over the coming years, these guideposts will start to function more *as a rule of law*–ignore them at your peril! In other words, every expenditure should be made with an eye on your NPM, or Basket No. 3. Can you afford this expenditure or that, or a salary of $XXX for each member of your staff, and still maintain your necessary and appropriate profit margin, be it 25 percent, 30 percent, or 10 percent?

This is where being a good steward of equity becomes very practical. For example, while I frequently mention taking care of your stakeholders and paying a "living wage" throughout this book, that determination is yours as a small business owner to make. Society and your employees may have an opinion, but they don't get to determine how much they are paid in order to live the lifestyle they want; this is an ownership decision. Bluntly, you only have so much money to spend per month and a profit goal to meet. The good news is that utilizing the tools of growth and efficiency, you can solve these problems over time.

If you determine through experience and/or benchmarking and/or the advice of your accountant that, for example, 20 percent profitability for your business in your location is indeed reasonable, competitive, and is to be your annual goal, then work back to Basket No. 1 and figure out how much you can afford to spend on wages for the staff members. If you are underpricing your business's services or goods, then fix that problem and adjust your performance ratios. If you are not able to reprice your goods or services due to competitive pressure, which is a common result, then after reasonable ownership compensation is paid, you will know what you have available for staff wages and benefits. I'll add that *reasonable* owners' compensation is an integral part of this process. Here is why all this matters.

From an appraiser's and an investor's point of view, your NPM is the starting point for building a valuable, investable business. Annual gross revenue is often the primary measurement tool for success relied on by sole proprietorships. Profits, or profitability, is the primary measurement tool for business owners through an entity structure. Profits, or what's left after all expenses and at least reasonable compensation to the owner(s) has been paid, is what investors are interested in because profits support growing share value and answer the question, "Where does the money come from for a key employee to buy in?" Profits are also one of the key factors that a next generation investor's bank looks to when considering a conventional or SBA loan to support such an investment. This is the attribute of being lendable. Small businesses, in order to be good stewards of equity (Tier One), must be competitively profitable. Period.

Overhead expenses, to a large degree, are the most difficult category to significantly reduce or change, though this cash flow category certainly warrants a firm hand at all times. A lower profitability picture might appear as performance ratios of 70/20/10, applying our Three-Basket Cash Flow System. Again, I'll concede that almost everything works as to Basket No. 2 with an ownership team limited to the founder or founders, since their base wages are augmented by the profits flowing through Basket No. 3, at least in the tax conduit models utilized in these explorations. The ownership level can simply decrease the amount of cash through Basket No. 2 and effectively increase the amount of cash through Basket No. 3, within reason, as it all flows through to the owners pro rata. But while that might provide a short-term solution, it is not a good, long-term strategy. Here is a better way to think about your business as you form your operational and cash flow goals.

2.5.1. A hypothetical. Let's say that you decide that your small business ("Newco") is to be an exemplary steward of your internal stakeholders. You want to provide living wages and benefits that are well above what your competitors seem to be providing so you can attract and retain the best talent to help you. The result is that you are able to generate consistent profitability of 10 percent and you do so purposefully, and proudly. Think of this as a 60/30/10 set of performance ratios. How could this profitability level, or NPM, affect your value as an owner, and the business's investability to a key employee/next gen investor or third-party?

A 10% profit margin can have a nuanced effect on the value and investability of a small business like Newco. It is not inherently good or bad without considering the broader context. Here's a breakdown of how it might be positively perceived for such a business that has demonstrated good stewardship to its internal stakeholders:

- Sustainability and viability: A 10 percent profit margin indicates that the business is generating more revenue than its total expenses, suggesting a sustainable and viable business model. This is a fundamental requirement for any investor.

- Reinvestment potential: Profits allow Newco to reinvest in various aspects of the business, such as product development, marketing, expanding operations, or improving sustainability initiatives. This reinvestment can drive future growth and increase long-term value.

- Attractiveness to certain investors: For investors focused on being a good steward and steady, sustainable growth rather than hyper-growth, a 10 percent profit margin might be attractive. It suggests a balanced and purposeful approach and responsible financial management.

- Valuation multiple: Profit margins are a key component in many business valuation methods. While the specific multiple applied would depend on various factors (industry, growth rate, risk), a healthy profit margin generally supports a higher valuation.

- Demonstrates efficiency: A 10 percent profit margin, especially in a small business than can demonstrate a strong record of ongoing stewardship on behalf of all its stakeholders, can signal that Newco, is managing its costs effectively and operating efficiently within its market, while attracting and retaining the best talent to support future growth.

Potential negative impacts or considerations for value and investability:

- Growth potential: Depending on the industry and market, a 10 percent profit margin might be seen as moderate. Investors seeking high-growth opportunities might prefer businesses with higher profit margins that can fuel rapid expansion.

- Industry benchmarks: The attractiveness of a 10 percent profit margin depends heavily on the typical margins within the particular industry, profession, or line of work, especially for companies with a focus on durability. If competitors are achieving significantly higher margins, it could raise questions about Newco's pricing strategy, cost structure, or market positioning.

- Investment stage: For a very early-stage startup, a 10 percent profit margin might be excellent. However, for a more mature small business, investors might expect a higher return on their investment.

- Opportunity cost: Investors always consider the opportunity cost of investing in one business versus another. If similar businesses in the same sector offer higher profit potential, Newco might be less attractive to some investors.

- Economic conditions: In a strong economy, investors might expect higher profit margins. Conversely, in a downturn, a stable 10 percent margin might be seen as more resilient.

"A man sets out to draw the world. As the years go by, he peoples a space with images: kingdoms, mountains, bays, ships, islands, fishes, rooms, instruments, stars, horses, and people. A short time before he dies, he discovers that the patient labyrinth of lines traces the image of his own face."

Jorge Luis Borges
(Argentina)

Of course, the size, age, and revenue level of a business also makes a difference as to these perspectives. A small business with eighty employees (or more) that has been in business for twenty-plus years and has a strong track record in terms of growth, stewardship, and reputation will be looked at far differently than a business one-fifth the size and age with the same profit margin.

A 10% profit margin for Newco is likely a positive indicator of a durable business. However, its impact on value and investability depends on a multitude of factors, including industry benchmarks, growth potential, the specific goals of potential investors, and the unique characteristics of Newco's business model and market. To get a more precise understanding, investors would likely conduct thorough due diligence, comparing Newco's financial performance against its peers, analyzing its growth trajectory, and evaluating its long-term strategic plan. They would also consider the qualitative aspects of the business, such as its brand, management team, and commitment to its values.

One argument I'd put forward is that by making a substantial investment in its support team, Newco should be poised for stronger, sustainable growth through innovation superior products and services. This growth, with an eye on Basket No. 1 in the future, should improve Newco's profit margins and market share. Time will tell.

2.5.2. The plateau level compensation strategy. This is where equity comes into the picture. The challenge and the opportunity to significantly adjust your cash flow model for long-term success and profitability comes when (preferably next generation) key employees seek to become investors and join the ownership team. To work through this process, we'll need to implement some new, basic terminology. Each generation of ownership will be referred to as follows:

- G1 = Generation One

- G2 = Generation Two

- G3 = Generation Three

The thinking isn't that we need a parent/child generational sequencing, but the math does require about a twelve to fifteen year age difference between G1 and G2, and subsequently, G2 and G3. Buying equity with after-tax dollars, with interest, fueled by growth, simply takes time.

A firm rule to understand is that new, younger owners won't buy equity, take the responsibility for a seven- to ten-year promissory note, *and take a pay cut*. Whatever wages they have enjoyed recently as employees, including any recurring annual bonus, will generally translate into their full wages as an owner more times than not. As such, a new owner's entrance into the equation tends to reset all the cash flow numbers, starting with Basket No. 2, and it usually turns out to be a good thing over time. Let's examine that premise in more depth.

Consider what happens when G2(A), a key employee, acquires equity in your business. G2(A) stops being an expense (no disrespect intended) and shifts over from Basket No. 1 to Basket No. 2 with you and any other G1(s)—their wages all come out of this second, more readily controllable cash flow basket. At this point, however, there are more changes than might be immediately apparent. Basket No. 2 wages, for example, do not need to change every year thereafter, or at least not much. Owners have more ways, and better ways, of being paid and building wealth than just wages plus a bonus, all at ordinary income tax rates–including stock appreciation over time in a growing business and, in some jurisdictions, a tax savings on profit distribution dollars. Bonuses are not a common way to compensate owners/investors and that process typically comes to an end for G2(A).

Applying a stabilizing approach to Basket No. 2 wages *for all owners*, what is called a *plateau level compensation strategy*, has the effect of freezing owners' compensation for three or four years at a time. This strategy is part of helping new, younger investors learn to think like owners and focus on growing the business they've invested in, watching general overhead expenses carefully, and increasing profits through smart, efficient growth. Growth is a major part of a small business's wealth building process for equity owners, new and old.

The reason that you should consider this approach and freeze all the owners' compensation levels (noting that owners can and should be paid different salaries based on their tenure, roles, and other factors) is because of the combined effects of profit distributions and growth in an increasingly efficient cash flow structure. As your small business continues to grow on the shoulders of more owners, with everyone watching general overhead in Basket No. 1, and with Basket No. 2 stabilized for several years, where do the new growth dollars go? In the years ahead, a portion of the new growth dollars will be allocated to Basket No. 1, for sure, but not all of them. By directing little to no new growth dollars into Basket No. 2, profitability should improve as most of the money goes straight to the bottom line, or NPM. In sum, this approach helps to reset the cash flow system and enables a business to grow through any profitability issues and strengthen the NPM over time—using equity as a tool.

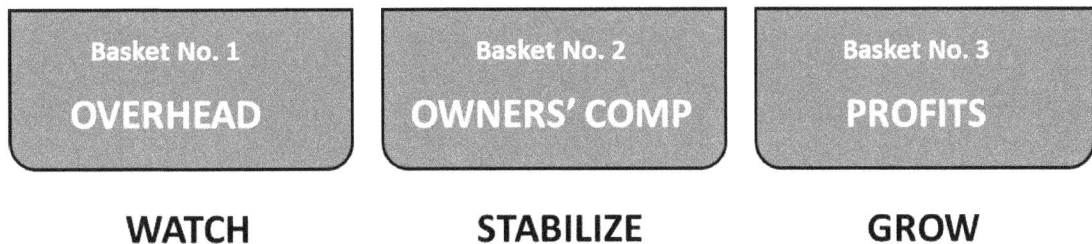

Basket No. 1	Basket No. 2	Basket No. 3
OVERHEAD	**OWNERS' COMP**	**PROFITS**
WATCH	**STABILIZE**	**GROW**

Figure 7

And it can get even better. At least in the U.S., many small business owners utilize an S corporation structure. This business model can reduce taxes on the dollars flowing through Basket No. 3, assuming at least reasonable compensation is paid through Basket No. 2. This leads to a natural tendency, with relatively equal levels of ownership, to *overweight* Basket No. 3 as the business continues to grow and settles the allocations as to the first two cash flow baskets. In the background, the higher profits support a higher business value, and that value tends to increase over time with growth, i.e., stock appreciation.

As a result, I have observed a number of highly valuable professional service models that have successfully implemented cash flow systems such as 30/30/40, or sometimes even 30/20/50, over a number of years, to take full advantage of these tax efficiencies.

That said, this book is intended for global readership—good small business stewards should know no boundaries! If your country offers a similar entity structure with tax benefits, talk to your accountant about your best choice. Understand that the U.S. based S corporation's tax benefit is helpful, but it doesn't make or break the cash flow process or compensation strategies we have explored. There are many other more important elements.

If your profession lies in a higher overhead model and you start this process at 50/40/10, imagine the impact by shifting two key employees into ownership through a purchase or a tax-neutral exchange and steadily moving towards a 40/40/20 cash flow system. Doubling the level of profitability will significantly impact the value of your business and make it more investable and lendable. Paying for equity, after taxes, with interest, tends to be a strong motivator to next gen owners/investors to grow the business they are relying on for their own futures.

This restructured cash flow system encourages the formation of *a team of colleagues* who rely on each other to service a collective client base, building value in a single enterprise designed to last for more than one generation. When a key employee, son, or daughter weigh the opportunity to purchase equity in the business where they work, they need to see several years of formal profit and loss statements and observe the historical overhead of the business. They need to see how much the owners have been and are currently paid for the work that they do, and the amount of profit dollars *actually distributed* to the owners over that time. Stock appreciation matters as well, though it does not provide annual cash flow as a benefit. The point is that you cannot do this on the eve of pitching the opportunity to one or more next generation investors or key employees.

Understand that even if you can increase the amount of money allocated to and paid out from Basket No. 3, it does not automatically increase the value of your business beyond a certain point. Appraisers, lenders, and investors will reevaluate your cash flow numbers in light of industry norms, a function referred to as normalizing cash flow. Normalizing a business's cash flow to reallocate *more appropriately* to the other two baskets, in hindsight, is done to make sure a business can actually be operated in a commercially reasonable and competitive manner. If you're a veterinarian and struggle to achieve 10 percent profitability, suddenly doubling Basket No. 3 by halving Basket No. 2 may well be met with the same normalizing approach, at least to some extent. The takeaway here is that the Three-Basket Cash Flow System can work any way you'd like when you're the only person it has to serve; once you have investors, things will change to benefit the entire group of owners. That is usually a good thing.

The concept of shareholder value, explored in the next section, will help you look at these cash flow basket allocations and your small business's performance ratios from a different angle, sharpening your focus on what it takes to be a great steward of equity on behalf of your internal stakeholders.

STEWARDSHIP SPOTLIGHT

TOO GOOD TO GO (COPENHAGEN, DENMARK): Too Good To Go was founded in 2015 in Copenhagen by a group of young entrepreneurs who shared a dream: to tackle the massive amounts of food wasted by buffet restaurants in Denmark. Driven by passion and urgency, they set out to create a simple but powerful tool—an app that would connect food businesses with individuals who wanted to rescue good food, help combat climate change, and save money at the same time.

The central purpose of the Too Good To Go app is to prevent edible surplus food from being discarded. Food waste is a major contributor to greenhouse gas emissions, as decomposing food releases methane, one of the most potent greenhouse gases. By rescuing food that would otherwise be wasted, Too Good To Go directly helps reduce these emissions, while creating a win-win scenario for businesses and consumers alike.

Today, Too Good To Go operates in 19 countries across Europe and North America with a thriving community of 100 million registered users and 175,000 active partner businesses. Yet the movement remains rooted in the original vision: that a small group of committed individuals can indeed make a real difference in the world through creative thinking, technology, and collective action.

2.6 MASTERING THE CONCEPT OF SHAREHOLDER VALUE

As we progress through these cumulative business building and strengthening steps, the concept of shareholder value must be added next as it demonstrates the broad package of ownership benefits derived by being good stewards of equity. In fact, this is probably the most compelling argument for taking the risk of ownership, and, conversely, for building a business that is valuable, profitable, and investable. This is equity at work. The basic formula expressing shareholder value is this:

**WAGES + PROFIT DISTRIBUTIONS + EQUITY
INCOME + STOCK APPRECIATION**

This formula states that, as a shareholder or owner, you can or should receive from your small business, wages for the work that you do (Basket No. 2), profit distributions as a return on your investment (Basket No. 3), income from the gradual, incremental sale of your stock over time as you allow younger owners to buy in to ownership (perhaps as part of a formal succession plan), all while the stock you own continues to appreciate in value as the business grows with the help of an expanding and motivated team. This is powerful. This is ownership level thinking. This is how you build wealth as a founder and use your business as a force for good for your stakeholders. Equity is how one gains access to these benefits.

Now let's add in some important tax basics because even small efficiencies, and inefficiencies, matter over the life of a durable, growing business. As a sole proprietor or a single owner LLC taxed as a disregarded entity, all the money that flows home from the work that you do, after expenses are deducted, is taxed as ordinary income. Effectively, this is a *two-basket cash flow model*, with Basket No. 1 used for general overhead expenses and Basket No. 2 used for wages *and* profits which, in a sole proprietorship, are taxed at the same ordinary income rate. That's not good and should be avoided if possible by using a flow-through entity structure.

Taking this to a higher level, let's overlay the shareholder value formula with tax efficiencies. This will provide an important and different perspective on how your business can begin to work for you as a founding owner. Assume that your entity structure includes an S corporation (this could be a basic S corporation, or an LLC electing to be taxed as an S corporation). In most states, owners receive wages for the work they do (at ordinary income rates on a W2 basis), plus profits for the ownership or equity they hold (at slightly less than ordinary income rates), plus sale proceeds at long-term capital gains (LTCG) tax rates less any basis (i.e., equity income) even as your business continues to grow with the help of the new, next generation owner(s), which is stock appreciation. Stock appreciates tax free until one day it is sold and the value is realized, at least in the U.S. Those are four different tax rates, three at less than ordinary income rates, as money and wealth are created and realized by those who own or acquire equity.

"The world would be happier if each person had the ability to be less complicated."

Clarice Lispector
(Brazil)

And there's more to this shareholder value concept. As your business's succession plan progresses, the assumption is that as you get older, you will gradually work fewer hours in the business. This assumption is based not only on observation and common sense but also on the need to forge a strong successor team. In a succession plan, the clientele of the business, as well as your staff members, need to see the next gen minority owners gradually assuming more of the day-to-day responsibilities. Having the founder(s) spend a little more time out of the office and trusting and training the next generation owners to supervise the operations in their absence is, ironically, a necessary part of the business perpetuation process. Think about this in the context of realizing the other four shareholder value benefits over the last ten to fifteen years of your career.

If, as a founding owner, you are willing to seller finance your next generation owners as they incrementally acquire your equity, the shareholder value formula looks even better:

WAGES + PROFIT DISTRIBUTIONS + EQUITY INCOME + INTEREST INCOME + STOCK APPRECIATION

As a founding owner slowly reduces their hours worked, there is a strong tendency for their wages (Basket No. 2) to plateau indefinitely and even gradually decline over time. In a growing business, even as the founder's wages plateau or decline in the latter part of the plan, the founder's profit distributions should continue to climb (in actual dollars rather than as a percentage of equity owned), as well as their stock price since the younger owners are using smart, efficient growth to fuel their own debt service and recoup their investment in the business. Note that the income stream at the highest tax rate to the founding owner(s) is the first to be eroded; that's not a coincidence. The founding or senior owner(s) has other ways, and better ways, to get the money home! This is making the business work for you and your stakeholders.

The idea is that next generation owners/buyers will use most, but not all, of their profit distributions to service the debt on the stock they bought as, ideally, multiple owners help to grow the business revenues. We generally assume that a younger prospective owner's current wages are already spoken for, so this new, slightly more tax-efficient revenue stream is used to pay down the debt. As the business grows and the profit dollars increase, the debt servicing can accelerate even as the value of the stock they hold grows tax free, at least in the U.S. That shifts the basic formula for the G2 and G3 owners to this:

WAGES + PROFIT DISTRIBUTIONS – DEBT SERVICE + STOCK APPRECIATION

So why does this matter? As a business and its ownership team learn to become good stewards and support their stakeholders, internal and external to the business, profits play an outsized role. Profits matter for many reasons and to many people. As a business owner myself, I take issue with those who say that being a good steward means that you should not prioritize or maximize business profits. That sounds noble to say, but practically, it makes little sense. Without strong, consistent profitability, especially in a small business, there are no next generation investors. Without the next gen owners, the business and its role in making the world a better place comes to an end. And it takes a long time for a new business to restart and gain enough momentum to make a significant difference. Something to think about.

STEWARDSHIP SPOTLIGHT

VAUDE (TETTNANG, GERMANY): VAUDE is a German producer of high-quality mountain sports equipment, founded in 1974 by Albrecht von Dewitz. This family-owned company, based in southern Germany, is committed to maintaining high ecological and social standards across its global supply chains. VAUDE ensures that its products are manufactured under fair working conditions and prioritizes transparency through certifications such as the Green Button, the Fair Wear Foundation, and its own Green Shape label.

Leadership of the company has passed to Albrecht's daughter, Antje von Dewitz, who has continued to deepen VAUDE's environmental and social commitments while expanding its global impact. Under her leadership, VAUDE has become a model for purpose-driven businesses, embracing sustainability, climate protection, and stakeholder well-being.

Through initiatives like VAUDE Second Hand, an online shop for pre-owned gear, and VAUDE Rent, a rental program for outdoor equipment, the company offers customers more sustainable ways to enjoy the outdoors. These programs reduce the environmental impact of overproduction and promote a circular economy by extending product life.

VAUDE's philosophy is both simple and smart: as long as a product can still be used, there's no need to make a new one.

2.7 UNDERSTANDING BUSINESS VALUE AND VALUATION

MOST SMALL BUSINESS OWNERS HAVE some idea of what their business is worth, though most estimates are based on relatively simple rules of thumb which look at just one of many variables and try to draw a useful conclusion. Frankly, I did that all the time in my own professional services business just to keep a sense of perspective—and most of the time, it made me feel good or at least informed without having to hire and pay an appraiser. At the same time, I would never have been able to sell stock or obtain a bank loan or obtain a key-man insurance policy using *my number* without a formal business appraisal and an objective opinion.

It's a bit like checking the weather. Most days, you can glance out the window wherever you may live, feel the breeze, see the clouds, and dress accordingly. But if you are planning a flight, a mountain ascent, or a high-stakes outdoor event, you want and need satellite data, radar models, and professional forecasts. The level of precision you need depends entirely on the decision you're trying to make.

The only way to know what your business is worth *for the specific purpose you have in mind* is to have it valued by a professionally qualified and objective appraiser. Everything else is just a guess. And there will be a difference of opinion between owner and appraiser, and next gen equity buyer/investor and appraiser—count on it. And there will be a difference of opinion between an owner and a prospective next gen investor, even with an appraisal—count on that too. Like it or not, every owner, current and prospective, needs to know the facts and the valuation logic at some point as applies to what they are building or buying into. An informed, objective opinion helps to level the field.

The first thing to know is that a small business as we've defined the term (100 or fewer owners and employees combined) doesn't have just one value, and there is no single valuation approach or method that can be applied to every situation or to every business. Just like with your car, value depends on *the purpose* of the valuation. Are you valuing your car to sell it to a third-party? To trade it in? Are you donating it to charity? Are you liquidating the asset at or near the end of its useful life? Depending on the purpose, your car has many different values across a wide range, and the values can all be correct. Business valuations work the same way.

Let's start this discussion in the same place most small business owners start–the practical and simpler side of things. Small business owners often *self-value* using a gross revenue multiple, or GRM, which is a rule of thumb. One specific example of a GRM is valuing a small business at 1.5 x T-12 (trailing twelve months) gross revenue. The GRM in this example is 1.5, and depending on your specific profession, GRMs might range from 0.75 up to 3.0 x T-12. With a bit of research, you should be able to find an applicable GRM for your specific business or line of work, or perhaps an applicable, narrow range of multiples. The best way to arrive at a semi reliable GRM is to find several recently completed, similar transactions and simply do the math (the final total sales price divided by the gross revenue)—if you can find the transaction details. Your attorney and/or accountant might be good sources of information on this front.

Back in my day as an attorney with a small practice, I sold for a GRM of 1.0 x T-12. That was the commonly applied standard at the time. By the way, even if using a relatively simple rule of thumb, it would be wise to use a T-36 approach—you'll get a much clearer picture of a business's performance over thirty-six months than just twelve months.

A GRM is often used on smaller cash flow streams, think $200,000 to $350,000/ year or less, where the logic lies somewhere between "How wrong can I be?" and "I'm not paying someone $8,000 to tell me what I already know." Smaller businesses in this gross revenue range normally do not sell or transfer their expenses and liabilities to an outside or third-party buyer; that and the lower revenue sometimes negates the need for an appraisal. Profits or profitability often are not the defining result for such sized businesses. And even if you own a larger and more sophisticated business and you just want to satisfy your curiosity, a GRM appropriate for your line of work may be good enough. An earnings-based multiple is probably more appropriate for a small business above $500,000/year, or certainly a business that endeavors to be a good steward of equity (Tier One) and follows the logic we've explored thus far in Part Two of this book.

Just to be real clear, when it comes to selling equity or stock, a small business owner is rarely justified in seizing the highest and simplest valuation result from the realm of possibilities or a range of multiples, no matter how unique and special your business might be. If you are going to be a good steward of equity, you will need to hire an appraiser at some point and consider the logic that these professionals apply. You may not like their opinion, but you need to understand why they think the answer is $X,XXX,XXX.00.

Let's put business value and valuation into perspective. Think back to the Three-Basket Cash Flow System where we examined how a strong business might bring as much as 25 percent (or more) of annual gross revenue to the bottom line of your P&L (profits) after all expenses and owners' compensation has been paid. Using $2,000,000 in gross revenue, this leaves $500,000 in actual profits, i.e., Basket No. 3, or your net profit margin (NPM).

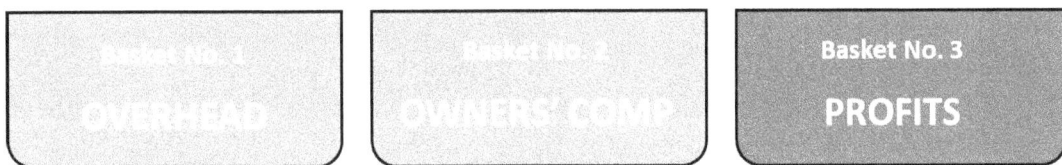

Basket No. 1	Basket No. 2	Basket No. 3
OVERHEAD	OWNERS' COMP	**PROFITS**

Figure 8

Profitability is the starting point for determining value. Annual gross revenue is often the primary measurement tool for success relied on by sole proprietorships or smaller, simpler one-owner entities, while profits are the primary measurement tool for small business owners focused on equity stewardship. Profitability (NPM) is what investors are interested in because profits support growing share value. Starting here, let's talk about the conceptual valuation differences between selling equity internally to one or more key staff members and one day selling the entire business to an external third-party buyer.

"The growing good of the world is partly dependent on unhistoric acts."

George Eliot
(England)

Being a good steward of equity means helping next generation owners purchase a noncontrolling equity interest. Acquiring an equity stake necessarily includes the existing profit and loss statement and the existing balance sheet. New key employee owners are buying expenses and liabilities. For these reasons, among others, the profits of $500,000 earned from $2,000,000 in gross revenue in this continuing example **are generally valued in the range of four to six times profitability or**

EBITDA (earnings before interest, taxes, depreciation, and amortization), again using a simple, rule-of-thumb multiple of earnings for illustration purposes. This is a rough valuation for the entire business, then to be multiplied by the amount of equity being purchased (i.e., 10%). Of course, your business's specific profession or occupation, location, competition, niche, and growth rates also matter.

Let's compare and contrast selling equity internally and incrementally to selling the entire business to a third-party buyer, again using simple guidelines to make an important point clear. A complete sale of a business usually permits a stronger, larger buyer to avoid acquiring the business's expenses and liabilities and, when structured correctly, the buyer can also write off or depreciate the entire purchase price over time. These are some significant advantages over a younger, next generation buyer/investor, especially an employee with little personal capital to invest. The result is that buyers or acquirers in a competitive acquisition setting **often pay a multiple of earnings of between seven to nine times profitability or EBITDA**, at least in the U.S.

There are two important takeaways to consider. One is the need to shift to a profit mentality for value and valuation purposes. For a growing, valuable, profitable, investable business, GRMs do not apply and are not really helpful–GRMs ignore too many important factors. And two, you knew it was coming, but here is the caveat. These relatively narrow valuation ranges and specific rules of thumb are simply not reliable across the vast spectrum of business models and venues and locations. This is a learning exercise, and the concepts are sound; but real numbers depend on specific facts and details and circumstances. Remember the valuation concepts as you begin your own journey towards long-term success.

To that end, and to complete the circle, there is one question that needs to be answered. Why would a founding owner want to sell some of their equity to a key employee, son or daughter, or other investor for a four times or five times EBITDA multiple in many cases when they could sell at a seven times or eight times multiple through an external sale? The answer starts with our shareholder value formula, but this time with the emphasis on results achieved over at least ten years, even as the founder gradually turns over their workload to their next gen successor team:

WAGES + PROFIT DISTRIBUTIONS + EQUITY INCOME + STOCK APPRECIATION

A founding owner who starts the equity stewardship process early enough can enjoy the cumulative benefits of wages, profits, equity income and stock appreciation, and the accompanying tax efficiencies, all while reducing time in the office or store over ten to twenty years, maybe longer. Most founders (nine out of ten in my experience) find this approach, along with being able to retain control longer, to be cumulatively more lucrative than selling for a lump sum at a higher multiple to an outside buyer and walking away. That, of course, is a call only you can make.

A few last thoughts:

a) The level of profitability dictates business value; those same profits are used to service the debt when next gen owners/key employees buy in. That is not a coincidence.

b) Most business owners do not have any experience with the business appraisal process; a home appraisal is completely different. The only way to know what a business is worth for the purpose you have in mind is to have it valued by a qualified, objective appraiser.

c) There is no equity to sell in a sole proprietorship, only the assets of the business.

STEWARDSHIP SPOTLIGHT

WHO GIVES A CRAP (MELBOURNE, AUSTRALIA): Probably best to let these folks tell you directly what their business is about, so please visit their website at https://us.whogivesacrap.org/pages/about-us. The point is clear: roughly 40 percent of the global population still lacks access to a toilet, which means that around 289,000 children under five die every year from diarrheal diseases caused by poor water and sanitation. That's nearly 800 children per day — or one child every two minutes.

In July 2012, Simon Griffiths, Jehan Ratnatunga, and Danny Alexander launched Who Gives A Crap. They delivered their first toilet paper products in March 2013 and have been growing steadily ever since. True to their mission, the company donates 50 percent of its profits to building toilets and improving sanitation in the developing world.

Who Gives A Crap is a Certified B Corporation® and holds FSC® Chain-of-Custody certification for responsible sourcing. Their sustainable business model has earned them top environmental ratings from independent evaluators, and in 2024, the brand was recognized as Australia's top corporate giver.

2.8 GENERATING STRONG, CONSISTENT GROWTH

THE CONCEPT IS RELATIVELY SIMPLE: multiple generations of motivated owners working together, each with a unique skill set, are capable of generating higher revenue growth over a longer period than a single, experienced founder, or even a small group of founding owners. It is the execution of the concept that is sometimes complex!

Thus far in Part Two, we've talked about how to make your small business more valuable and investable. The answers are a combination of profitability and growth through an organized cash flow system in the proper entity structure. In terms of growth, to be specific, this means that the business is fueled by steady, strong, top line revenue growth (i.e., gross revenue). Ideally, this growing revenue stream is accompanied by greater efficiencies, or scale, as well. But make no mistake, growth is imperative.

Revenue growth rates work well as a measure of success from one year to the next for most small businesses. Even though much of our focus in building a valuable, investable, and durable business is on profitability, gross revenue numbers are important too. These results are typically available to all founders even from their days as sole proprietorships, and tracking such revenue growth over increments of three to five years is highly informative to an owner, current or prospective. This is why we expanded our working terminology to include Gross Profit Margin (GPM) and Operating Profit Margin (OPM).

If a business increases its gross revenue from $1,000,000 to $2,000,000 over a five-year period, that equates to a CAGR (compound annual growth rate) of 14.9 percent/year. The calculation process of a CAGR requires three inputs: (1) the beginning value, (2) the ending value, and (3) the period. A CAGR takes into account the effect of compounding, which means that your business revenue growth builds upon itself, another powerful tool in the hands of a well-informed small business owner and forecaster. To calculate your CAGR over any period you choose, just use one of the many free and readily available online calculators built for this purpose–a simple way to calculate a very important number.

Let's talk about why revenue growth matters, especially to an investing next gen owner who might be a current key employee and/or your son or daughter. I met a gentleman midway through my career who owned a professional services business in the field of wealth management and insurance. He led a successful team for over four decades, and when he sold the last of his equity to his three next gen owners at age seventy-five and retired with an appraised business value of more than $25 million, he told me his simple philosophy that he frequently shared with his successor team, one of whom was his son: "If a small business doesn't grow by at least 15 percent a year, top line, it's dying." Take that for what it is worth. As a business owner, this was my personal benchmark.

Growth is particularly important in the internal stewardship process, though it does not require a 15 percent CAGR into perpetuity to make everything work. Strong, steady, profitable growth is the goal. Predictability matters to those who are or will be investors. A simple and effective way to approach the growth process and to set goals for the business is to calculate how long it will take for your business to double in value, especially with help from additional owner(s) and perhaps some innovative thinking as a team.

The time to double in size is seventy divided by the constant annual growth rate you are targeting. This is about setting goals or additional guideposts for the journey ahead. For instance, consider an annual target growth rate of 10 percent. According to the *rule of 70*, it will take seven years (70/10) for the quantity to double. At an annual growth rate of 15 percent, your business will double in value in just over four and a half years (70/15 = 4.67). The similar *Rule of 72* is considered more accurate for higher growth rates (typically 10 percent or more) and is easily divisible by more numbers. This is thinking about where your business is going or where you want it to go. How you get there is a different matter.

There is a common misperception by smaller business builders and owners (e.g., sub $1,000,000 in gross annual revenues) that a gross revenue growth rate of 10 percent to 15 percent is increasingly unsustainable as a business grows larger and larger. In other words, the thinking is that it is easier to grow faster year over year when you are smaller or your revenues are less. Having been there and done that, I would argue the opposite. In fact, as a business gets larger, it can and should develop a stronger and deeper bench of talent—people you probably couldn't afford or even attract as a fledgling small business or as a sole proprietorship. A small business has the ability, for example, to invest specifically in marketing and sales professionals instead of fully tasking individual owners and key employees to be the primary revenue generators.

"Do not seek to follow in the footsteps of the wise; seek what they sought."

Matsuo Basho
(Japan)

As a result, with growth and experience, a business's leadership should have the funds to hire key staff members who *actually have education, skills, and experience* in marketing a small business in your specific venue. A larger business armed with a budget and clear, specific growth, marketing, and sales goals to achieve as a group is arguably much better positioned to consistently grow at higher levels and for longer periods of time than a similarly situated business that depends on singular, uncoordinated efforts. That has been my experience over the past thirty years.

I recognize that this philosophy runs counter to most owners' beliefs. But think about it for a moment. Many small businesses depend on a single or primary individual who attempts to serve as the head of client services, marketing and sales, HR, IT, and so on–the role of a founding owner. At some point, such an individual will simply *run out of gas*, or *hit a ceiling*, or whatever metaphor you would prefer. It is inevitable. Regardless, by age fifty-five or so, most founders who are still *forces of one* start to enjoy the results of their hard work and they begin to slow down and, justifiably, work less hard than they did in their thirties and forties. They can coast for a while, but eventually growth will suffer. Few next-generation employees or family members will invest in a business whose growth is securely tied to a single individual.

As your business grows and you think about adding another owner or two, the ability to scale it becomes increasingly important, and possible. Accept that it may well be the next generation of ownership who figures it out, *because they'll have to*. But if you are fortunate and smart about it, founding owners can at least start the process together with their successors and develop a strategic plan. Rarely have I seen the founding owner alone figure out the scalability issue before taking on new, next gen owners.

Some small business owners know this, but most do not, so let's address the basics first. Growth and scale are different issues. Most efforts to grow a business are focused primarily on top-line growth while watching overhead expenses carefully with the goal of maintaining a certain level of profitability. But, typically, increasing the gross revenue of a small business means increasing the expenses as well, often proportionally. Scalability is about growing the gross revenues disproportionately to the general overhead expenses of the business. It usually requires planning, funding, the right systems and processes, staff, technology, and partners. This can be hard to do in a small business, but it is almost always possible with a good plan and some high-level thinking.

The issue of scale first arises when strategies used in the past to grow stop working, or at least stop working efficiently or well. Most entrepreneurs reach a point where they simply can't work any harder or longer, and they cannot acquire and serve more clients. It feels like they need to expand the business, but any more growth feels impossible to sustain. At some point, there is just too much to do and not enough hours in the day to get it done. The common solution? Hire and train another person to do exactly what the founder and chief revenue producer does, or did. And then owners do that over and over again. The common result is that most small businesses do not become more profitable (as a percentage of gross revenue) as they get bigger.

Pause here for a moment, please. Scalability is a key step in building for long-term success. Making your business *work for you* means it can work for someone else, too, and then it becomes investable and valuable. Difficult as it may be, this is worth your time and attention.

Scale can be very elusive, and I think the problem often lies in entrepreneurial thinking, the very thing that helps every new owner survive in the early years of a new venture. As an entrepreneur, the first problem you have to solve is revenue. If the founding owner(s) can't make a living, they won't survive financially. But over time, an entrepreneur's confidence grows, and the myriad challenges and problems are solved using ingenuity, hard work, and even trial and error. At some point, however, problems like figuring out how to scale a business surpass one's basic entrepreneurial skills; working harder actually becomes part of the problem. I can attest to this from personal experience coming from a long line of workaholics and entrepreneurs.

Here are some suggestions to consider. First, growth is a common theme in a sustainable business, so apply the concept to the issue of adding scale. The challenge is immediate, but the solution is not—it will take time, perspective, and skill. If your business can sustainably grow at a 10 percent CAGR, in seven years it will double its revenue flow. So start now and scale *for that business*. Who will you need? What needs to change? What is missing? Start answering those questions now, lay out a plan, and grow into it. Building for long-term success will provide a number of important guideposts along the way and require some new thinking and some new or additional talent. If you double in size, you will have the budget to accommodate these changes.

Second, in your owners' and/or operational and planning meetings, memorialize your growth goals and *get specific* about what you want or need to achieve and the timetable for doing so. And then read, learn, and listen. Hire a coach with a proven record in helping other businesses like yours turn this corner. Consider hiring the talent you may not have and bring in new and better thinking on this subject matter. Study other businesses, even those from other professions and industries. Working harder isn't the answer to the question, maybe for the first time, so get smart about it. Ask for help. There are a lot of good books on scaling a small business. My job is mostly to make you aware that you need to do something about it.

Third, marketing and sales are common pinch points for small businesses that want to grow into valuable, profitable, durable businesses. This is because at the smaller and/or newer levels of business ownership, in many instances, the entrepreneur honestly believes that they are the best and only solution to obtain more clients and produce more revenue. Many owners, *forces of one*, think the answer lies in this approach: *Find another one of me. I am very good at what I do. Let's just keep doing what works. And if I can't do that, then I've grown as large as I can.* That thinking is wrong, with all due respect. Hiring experienced marketing and sales professionals and arming them with goals and a budget dedicated to bringing in new clients and a high level of annual growth is a step forward in the scalability process. The goal isn't always to get bigger; maybe it is time to get better.

STEWARDSHIP SPOTLIGHT

REET AUS (TALLINN, ESTONIA): Reet Aus is a pioneering fashion designer who produces clothing and accessories using preexisting textiles and garments. A PhD-qualified environmental activist and natural rebel, she founded the Reet Aus Collection® and is recognized as a leader in industrial upcycling for fashion.

(The textile and garment industry is one of the largest contributors to global waste and environmental degradation. Globally, it's estimated that more than 92 million tons of textile waste are generated each year—a number projected to reach over 130 million tons by 2030 if current trends continue.)

In her mission to create systemic change, Reet developed the Upmade® certification to help brands and factories implement scalable, sustainable upcycling processes. Her industrial method—known as "Upcycled by Reet Aus" or "U by Reet Aus"—transforms waste materials into products with higher value, better quality, or a new purpose, directly challenging the throwaway culture that dominates the global fashion industry.

Reet's guiding mission is clear: to save the fashion industry from itself by proving that sustainability and large-scale production can coexist. For her groundbreaking work, she has earned numerous awards, including being named one of the "Top 20 Responsible Leaders in Northern Europe."

2.9 BUILDING YOUR SUCCESSOR TEAM

A SUCCESSION PLAN INVOLVES MULTIPLE owners and multiple generations of ownership who work together to build a valuable, profitable, growing, and durable business. The basic formula to support this process is: G1 + G2 + G3, or more precisely, G1 + G2(x2) + G3(x3). This is called your successor team. Each generation (G1 = generation one, G2 = generation two compared to G1, and so on) of ownership tends to require a gradually broader base of ownership to support the buy-out costs of the more senior generation of owners in a valuable and growing business.

I want to be careful not to overthink the long-term success goal for you, though after eleven years of college, I may well be totally incapable. Succession planning can be complex. But if you own a small business that doubles in size several times over in a single generation of ownership, you're going to need some help to run it and take it into the next generation on behalf of your stakeholders. That's the simplest way to say it.

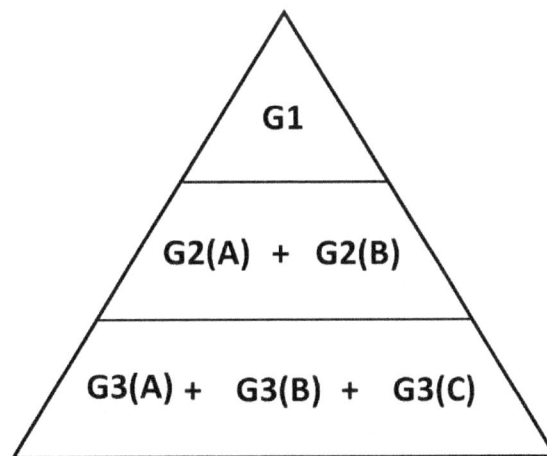

Figure 9

Most succession plans are incremental transfers of ownership with each equity acquisition step called a "tranche." A typical plan will have two or three tranches with each tranche requiring, on average, about 7 years to fully complete. Tranches often overlap, making the exact duration of a succession plan variable.

If a succession plan starts when G1, a founding owner, is fifty-three years of age, the basic math (including amortization schedules to support the after-tax equity buy-in process) suggests that two prospective next generation owners should ideally be in their mid- to late-thirties to provide the best results for long-term success. If G2(A) is thirty-four and G2(B) is thirty-eight, the G2s' average age of thirty-six is used for planning and modeling purposes. This is about a seventeen year average age difference compared to G1 in this simple example. Of course, there are other factors that come into play, so the math for each generational level of the plan depends on your specific situation. Bank lenders typically offer an amortization schedule of seven to ten years, and for good reason; this reflects the time needed to pay for equity after taxes out of the profit distributions received by the buyers of the stock.

Succession plans need to be custom designed and built to address each business's specific fact pattern and goals.

The exact number of G2 owners and G3 owners depends on the goals, timeframe, profitability level, growth rates, and the value of the business—and of course the pool of available next gen talent. The successor team is commonly composed of two or more younger owners who collectively (but not always equally) purchase ownership from the G1 level. In most cases, the process starts with a single key employee whose length of service (LOS) with the subject business is at least three to four years. It may be several years later that G1, while working with an existing G2, adds a second member to the successor team, and so on.

A good general guideline is two G2s for every owner in the G1 position when business value equals or exceeds $2.0 million, a pattern loosely repeated for the G3s, who will be tasked with being the successor team for the broader base of G2 owners. That said, two or three G2s can typically buy out two G1s in most cases with sufficient time and planning. Avoid having just one G2, or one person, on your successor team whose task is to buy out one or more G1 owners; it can work, but depending on business value, there may be little room for error, and the debt load, even when spread out over time on one individual buyer can be overwhelming and may result in a price paid that is lower, perhaps much lower, than fair market value (FMV).

To further the case for multiple next gen owners or successors, think about your business's contingency planning. Most small businesses with two or more owners use a buy-sell agreement to address sudden changes in the ownership team (death, disability, termination of employment status, loss of licensure, etc.). Consider the possibility that four or five years into G2's first purchase of a 10 percent equity stake, for example, and after the business has grown significantly, G1 has to buy out their only G2 owner for some reason. This succession plan has just shifted into reverse. G1 is now *buying* equity instead of selling it. The better approach is that each G2 owner needs to participate in a continuity plan that relies *on other G2 owners*. Beyond age fifty or so, it makes no sense for G1 (or any of the senior owners) to be acquiring equity from the younger owners, or any owner for that matter if the goal is to build a multi-generational business.

"The most precious gift we can offer anyone is our attention."

Thich Nhat Hanh
(Vietnam)

A new human resources or HR team also tends to emerge from the process of installing a successor team. As the succession plan gradually unfolds, and certainly by the time G2(s) acquires more equity in tranche two, the responsibility for hiring, training, and promoting next generation talent should begin to shift to the senior successor team members, with guidance from G1(s) of course. The G3 level of ownership will be the future business and continuity partners for G2, so it is important to let the G2 owners make some of these decisions; right or wrong, it's part of being an owner.

To this end, founding owners often struggle to find enough qualified, next generation talent to support their plan. The concern is often expressed as "How do I find people who will work as hard and care as much about my business as I do?" Which, in fairness, is a good question that must be asked and answered. In a growing and evolving business, however, the idea is that a team of next generation owners, each doing what they do best, can cumulatively succeed and supplant the entrepreneurial model where the founder does all or most of the important work, whether they are really good at it or not. G1 is replaced by the cumulative talents and efforts of the successor team, with G1 moving from entrepreneur to CEO, to mentor, retiring when they and the business and client base are ready. Over the decades, I've often been pleasantly surprised, and occasionally shocked, at the level of success and ingenuity these successor teams can generate as they propel the business to new heights.

How do you know if your key employee, son, or daughter is ready to be an owner? First, there should be a minimum amount of time that they work for you, three to four years at least. Second, don't make it too easy. New owners still need an investment mindset, and they need to feel the pressure of making such an important investment. When possible, let the banks do what banks do best and serve as the lender. One of the best ways to know if your key employee, son, or daughter is ready for the opportunity is to let them make the investment, sign a promissory note for a purchase of equity, and *write a check* on the first day of every month as they come to work and help grow the business, and their investment.

If you have a loyal, hardworking key employee who really makes a difference, it might make sense to have a conversation and talk about the opportunity and see what they think. You probably should do that sooner than later. Too many succession plans start *after* a key employee has left due to lack of opportunity.

If you're interested in learning more about setting up your own succession plan, either as a founder or an investor, please read one of my two previous books for the details:

- For G1s: *Building with the End in Mind: A Complete Succession Planning Guide for Professional Service Owners*

- For G2s/G3s: *Acquiring Your Future through a Succession Plan: A Primer for Next Gen Profession Service Professionals*

And those are the basic mechanics of building a business that can outlast you as the founder. Just remember, It's not enough to pass down a business; you have to pass down the principles that made it strong in the first place. That's how stewardship endures.

STEWARDSHIP SPOTLIGHT

BIOLITE (BROOKLYN, NEW YORK AND NAIROBI, KENYA): BioLite designs and produces off-grid energy products for outdoor recreation and emerging markets. The company is best known for its innovative wood-burning stoves that use thermoelectric technology to generate usable electricity from fire heat. Founded in 2006, BioLite operates as a for-profit small business with a clear mission: to empower people and protect the planet through access to renewable energy. Their vision is to provide clean energy access to 20 million people and avoid three million tons of CO_2e emissions by 2025.

BioLite's Emerging Markets (EM) Team, headquartered in Nairobi, Kenya, works closely with key partners across 23 countries to deliver last-mile distribution, training, and financing for remote customers. Their clean energy solutions—including smokeless stoves and solar lighting—significantly improve health, safety, and economic outcomes for families living in energy poverty, offering tangible benefits that go beyond simply providing products.

Meanwhile, BioLite also serves outdoor enthusiasts around the world, offering portable, reliable off-grid cooking, charging, and lighting solutions that enhance outdoor experiences while promoting more sustainable alternatives to traditional energy sources.

REFERENCES/PART TWO
(IN ALPHABETICAL ORDER):

BioLite. 2025. *Our Story and Impact.* BioLite Official Website. Accessed May 13, 2025. https://www.bio-liteenergy.com/pages/impact.

Grau Sr., JD, David. 2024. *Building With the End in Mind: A Complete Succession Planning Guide for Professional Service Owners.* Business Transitions Publishing, LLC.

Grau Sr., JD, David. 2025. *Acquiring Your Future Through a Succession Plan: A Primer for Next Generation Professional Service Providers.* Amazon Publishing, Barnes & Noble, Apple Books, et al.

Integrated Wealth Planning. 2025. *About Our Team and Philanthropy.* Integrated Wealth Planning Official Website. Accessed May 13, 2025. https://iwp-ky.com/our-team.

LAUDE the Label. 2025. *Our Ethical Production and Values.* LAUDE the Label Official Website. Accessed May 13, 2025. https://laudethelabel.com/pages/our-story.

Province Apothecary. 2025. *Our Story and Community Giving.* Province Apothecary Official Website. Accessed May 13, 2025. https://provinceapothecary.com/pages/our-story.

Reet Aus. 2025. *About Reet Aus and Upmade® Certification.* Reet Aus Official Website. Accessed May 13, 2025. https://www.reetaus.com.

soleRebels. 2025. *Our Story and Ethical Production.* soleRebels Official Website. Accessed May 13, 2025. https://www.solerebels.com/pages/our-story.

The Happy Pear. 2025. *About Us and Our Mission.* The Happy Pear Official Website. Accessed May 13, 2025. https://thehappypear.ie/about-us/.

Too Good To Go. 2025. *Our Story and Global Impact.* Too Good To Go Official Website. Accessed May 13, 2025. https://toogoodtogo.com/en-us/about-us.

VAUDE. 2025. *Our Commitment to Sustainability and Fairness.* VAUDE Official Website. Accessed May 13, 2025. https://www.vaude.com/en-INT/Company/.

Who Gives A Crap. 2025. *About Us and Our Impact.* Who Gives A Crap Official Website. Accessed May 13, 2025. https://us.whogivesacrap.org/pages/about-us.

PART THREE:
CHANGING THE WORLD

3.1 DEVELOPING A STEWARDSHIP PLAN

To successfully manage stakeholder relationships over the course of time, documenting the process is often necessary and helpful. A small business Stewardship Plan can be used to great effect. The point is that documenting the plan and involving your team members in that process goes beyond simple compliance or good intentions and demonstrates a strong commitment to long-term stewardship. Unlike a traditional business plan that focuses primarily on growth and profitability for shareholders, a Stewardship Plan emphasizes the responsible management of the business as an entity to be preserved and nurtured for future generations and for the benefit of a broader group of stakeholders. That is a message welcomed by all stakeholders.

Many small businesses will act on the principles of good stewardship without necessarily having a dedicated, detailed plan. For small businesses with five or fewer owners/employees, I think this is the norm—though one may still want to have at least a basic plan as outlined below. But as a small business grows larger and its footprint in a community increases in importance, the need to make stewardship an integral part of your business's culture will be aided by having a set of formal guidelines that everyone involved can reference and support. Certainly for small businesses with ten or more employees, having a formal Stewardship Plan becomes increasingly necessary to coordinate the various activities, cash flows, expenditures, and hiring practices, and to carefully align your business's mission, vision, and purpose with the everyday actions of your entire team. At some point, you can and should use your Stewardship Plan to attract and retain incoming talent, and your marketing team can share your specific principles and commensurate actions with your customers, suppliers, and community.

As you consider drafting your own formal Stewardship Plan (the "Plan"), let's work through an example that encompasses many of the issues and strategies you have read about thus far. This Plan is for a financial planning firm employing twelve people including the two current owners. This twelve-year-old small business is located in Riverview, a city of 250,000 people. Financial planning implies a professional services context in which client trust is paramount, a fiduciary interest exists, and long-term, even multi-generational planning is inherent. The goal of this Plan is good stewardship for all stakeholders. In addition, this Stewardship Plan specifically includes an ownership track and succession plan to ensure durability of the enterprise as the two current owners (who also serve as the managers and directors) are both in their early fifties.

After reading this basic plan, we will overlay it with additional components to simulate a common evolution of the document and this business's stewardship goals over time. Note that many of the ideas, concepts, and terms that you have read about in Parts One and Two will now begin to emerge in a single, unified Plan:

STEWARDSHIP PLAN for Riverview Financial Planning, LLC:

Date: March 27, 20__

A) **Our Purpose and Commitment.** Riverview Financial Planning, LLC is dedicated to providing exceptional financial planning services built on trust, integrity, and a long-term perspective. This Stewardship Plan outlines how we intend to operate responsibly toward our clients, our team, our community, and the future of the firm itself. This plan is integral to our mission and guides our daily decisions and actions.

B) **Core Principles.** We are committed to upholding the following principles in all aspects of our business:

1. **Client Stakeholder Group.**

   • Fiduciary Duty: Acting solely in the best interests of our clients.

- Transparency: Communicating clearly, honestly, and openly about our services, fees, and recommendations.

- Confidentiality: Protecting client information with the utmost care and security.

- Long-Term Relationships: Building enduring partnerships with clients based on mutual trust and understanding.

- Competence: Maintaining the highest levels of professional knowledge and skill. This firm will support and encourage everyone to obtain the necessary education and credentials to support our clients' needs and goals.

2. **Employee Stakeholder Group.**

- A Fair and Respectful Workplace: Being a leader in terms of compensation and benefits, fostering a positive and inclusive work environment, and treating every team member with respect.

- Professional Growth: Investing in the ongoing training, development, and credentialing of our team members.

- Work-Life Balance: Supporting the well-being of our employees by encouraging reasonable workloads and flexibility where possible.

- Clear Path for Advancement: Providing opportunities for career growth within the firm.

3. **Community Stakeholder Group.**

- Ethical Conduct: Operating with integrity and upholding the highest ethical standards in all our interactions.

- Local Engagement: Being a responsible corporate citizen, contributing positively to our local community, potentially through pro bono financial literacy efforts or support for local organizations.

- Responsible Resource Use: Operating our office efficiently to minimize waste and conserve resources. This firm's goal is to become a paperless office within five years.

4. **Firm (Business/Entity) Stakeholder Group (Ownership and Succession).**

- Continuity of Service: Ensuring the long-term stability and continuity of the firm for the benefit of our clients and employees through proactive succession planning.

- Internal Succession Priority: Prioritizing the development of internal talent for future leadership and ownership roles.

- Defined Ownership Track: Maintaining a clear, merit-based pathway for dedicated employees to achieve partnership and participate in the ownership equity of the firm. This includes mentorship and preparation for leadership responsibilities.

- Financial Prudence: Managing the firm's finances responsibly to ensure its long-term health and viability.

C) **Implementation and Accountability.**

1. Leadership Commitment: The current partners/owners are fully committed to upholding this Stewardship Plan.

2. Integration: These principles shall be integrated into our daily operations, client service standards, employee policies, and strategic planning.

3. Regular Review: Leadership will annually review this Plan to ensure its continued relevance and effectiveness.

D) **Conclusion.** Our commitment to stewardship ensures that Riverview Financial Planning, LLC not only provides outstanding financial guidance but also operates as a responsible, ethical, and sustainable firm for the long term. We believe this approach benefits our clients, empowers our team, strengthens our community, and secures the future legacy of this firm.

This basic Stewardship Plan provides clarity and focus, effectively addressing both broad stakeholder responsibility and the critical aspect of ownership succession planning for a personal services firm serving multiple generations of clients. This Plan, with minor modifications for your specific needs, goals, and occupation, could accommodate a wide variety of professional service small businesses including accounting, law, insurance, technology, health care, engineering, etc. It could also be adapted to just about any type of business with some overwriting and polishing. This is an excellent starting point and demonstrates how to make a formal stewardship commitment.

To enhance this learning experience, let's build on this Stewardship Plan and evolve it to make the community stewardship section *more specific* for this financial planning firm. The purpose of this exercise is to encourage consistent and focused stewardship and volunteer efforts within the community. As we consider how this Stewardship Plan could be improved in this area, what unique skills does a financial planning firm have that can benefit the community? For starters, I would list financial literacy, planning, and teaching the concepts of budgeting, saving, and setting retirement goals. In terms of a community outreach, many of these concepts apply to community members of all ages from high school students to senior citizens. Specific types of stewardship might include:

- Pro bono services (financial literacy workshops; one-on-one sessions, perhaps in concert with other financial planning businesses in the area; high school oriented financial basics)

- Employee volunteering (paid time off, organized group activities)

- Strategic partnerships (with specific nonprofits, schools, community centers)

- Financial support (sponsorships, donations)

- Board service (leveraging financial expertise)

- Local purchasing/sourcing

"Do the wise thing and the kind thing too,
and make the best of us and not the worst."

Charles Dickens
(England)

Next, I would suggest that this financial planning firm add *focused and consistent actions* to improve its Plan. Instead of doing a little of everything, perhaps inconsistently, choose one or two key areas as to each stakeholder group where the firm can make a meaningful impact, choosing areas that align with the firm's mission, vision, and purpose. Start small and keep it simple until those elements are a normal and natural part of the workweek and then consider adding more responsibilities and goals into the Plan. To this end, let's redraft two sections of the basic Stewardship Plan you just read and replace the more general points with specific, actionable commitments relevant to this small business (all changes are in **bold type**):

(MODIFIED) STEWARDSHIP PLAN for Riverview Financial Planning, LLC:

Date: March 27, 20__

A) Our Purpose and Commitment. Riverview Financial Planning, LLC is dedicated to providing exceptional financial planning services built on trust, integrity, and a long-term perspective. This Stewardship Plan outlines how we intend to operate responsibly towards our clients, our team, our community, and the future of the firm itself. This plan is integral to our mission and guides our daily decisions and actions.

B) Core Principles. We are committed to upholding the following principles in all aspects of our business:

1. Client Stakeholder Group.

- Fiduciary Duty: Acting solely in the best interests of our clients.
- Transparency: Communicating clearly, honestly, and openly about our services, fees, and recommendations.
- Confidentiality: Protecting client information with the utmost care and security.
- Long-Term Relationships: Building enduring partnerships with clients based on mutual trust and understanding.
- Competence: Maintaining the highest levels of professional knowledge and skill. This firm will support and encourage everyone to obtain the necessary education and credentials to support our clients' needs and goals.

2. Employee Stakeholder Group.

- A Fair and Respectful Workplace: Being a leader in terms of compensation and benefits, fostering a positive and inclusive work environment, and treating every team member with respect.
- Professional Growth: Investing in the ongoing training, development, and credentialing of our team members.
- Work-Life Balance: Supporting the well-being of our employees by encouraging reasonable workloads and flexibility where possible.

- Clear Path for Advancement: Providing opportunities for career growth within the firm.

3. Community Stakeholder Group **(Focusing on the Community of Riverview).**

- Ethical Conduct: Operating with integrity and upholding the highest ethical standards in all our interactions **within the Riverview community and beyond.**

- **Focused Local Engagement: We commit to actively engaging with and supporting the Riverview community through focused, consistent efforts that will include:**

  o **Financial Literacy Initiative: Dedicate firm resources (time and expertise) to improving financial literacy within the Riverview community. We will aim to deliver at least [e.g., two to four] financial wellness workshops annually, partnering with local schools, community centers, or nonprofits serving [e.g., young adults, seniors, or underserved populations—** *choose a focus***].**

  o **Strategic Nonprofit Partnership: Establish and maintain a long-term partnership with at least one specific Riverview-based nonprofit organization whose mission aligns with our firm's values. This partnership will involve [e.g., a combination of financial support, skills-based volunteering using our financial expertise, and/or board service].**

  o **Supported Employee Volunteerism: Encourage and support employee engagement in Riverview community initiatives by providing [e.g., eight to twelve hours] of paid volunteer time off (VTO) per employee annually, usable for firm-organized events or individual volunteering aligned with our focus areas.**

  o **Local Sourcing: Prioritize using local Riverview-area suppliers and vendors for office needs, catering, and events whenever practical and economically feasible.**

- Responsible Resource Use: Operating our office efficiently to minimize waste and conserve resources. This firm's goal is to become a paperless office within five years.

4. Firm (Business/Entity) Stakeholder Group (Ownership and Succession).

- Continuity of Service: Ensuring the long-term stability and continuity of the firm for the benefit of our clients and employees through proactive succession planning.

- Internal Succession Priority: Prioritizing the development of internal talent for future leadership and ownership roles.

- Defined Ownership Track: Maintaining a clear, merit-based pathway for dedicated employees to achieve partnership and participate in the ownership equity of the firm. This includes mentorship and preparation for leadership responsibilities.

- Financial Prudence: Managing the firm's finances responsibly to ensure its long-term health and viability.

C) Implementation and Accountability:

1. Leadership Commitment: The current partners/owners are fully committed to upholding this Stewardship Plan **and will champion community engagement efforts.**

2. Integration: These principles are integrated into our daily operations, client service standards, employee policies, and strategic planning.

3. **Coordination: [Optional: Designate a specific person or small rotating committee, e.g., "A designated partner" or "The operations manager"] will coordinate the financial literacy initiative and strategic nonprofit partnership activities. VTO will be managed through standard HR procedures.**

4. Regular Review: This plan, **including the progress of our community initiatives, will be reviewed annually by leadership to celebrate successes, identify areas for improvement, and reaffirm priorities for the coming year.**

D) Conclusion. Our commitment to stewardship ensures that Riverview Financial Planning, LLC not only provides outstanding financial guidance but also operates as a responsible, ethical, and sustainable firm for the long term. We believe this approach benefits our clients, empowers our team, strengthens our community, and secures the future legacy of this firm.

These additions provide concrete actions and targets, transforming the general principle of community engagement into a more focused and measurable aspect of the firm's stewardship efforts specifically directed at the community of Riverview. This structure makes it easier to track progress and ensure consistent effort year after year. Start simple with your own Stewardship Plan and gradually improve it, adding your preferences and passions into the document so that your team knows what your small business stands for, what ownership expects, and how they can help.

Here are a few additional suggestions focused on reinforcing your commitment and making your personal Stewardship Plan feel more integrated:

First, you could explicitly list your business's mission, vision, purpose and core values at the very beginning, perhaps just below the title or as part of Section A (Purpose and Commitment), if not included generally in the text. This serves to connect the specific stewardship actions back to the fundamental identity and values of your business, and it frames the plan not just as a set of actions but as a reflection of *who and what the firm is*.

Second, you might add an internal communication statement such as "This commitment will be shared with all team members upon hiring and reviewed annually in team meetings to ensure shared understanding and ongoing engagement. Our business's consistent and focused support of our community is part of who we are." This addresses how the plan lives within the firm beyond just being "another document." It reinforces that stewardship is part of the culture and is expected of everyone, without adding complex procedures.

Finally, you might add a short introductory paragraph to your Stewardship Plan in which the founder(s) personally speak to the importance of these commitments and to the firm's legacy and its role in the community. This adds a strong personal voice and reinforces leadership buy-in from the top. Here is an example:

A Message from the Founder(s)

When we first established [business name], our vision extended beyond simply building a successful [type of business]. We aimed to create an enduring firm deeply rooted in integrity, one that would not only serve our clients with unwavering dedication but also foster the growth of our team and contribute meaningfully to the fabric of this community we call home. This Stewardship Plan, therefore, is more than a set of guidelines; it is a personal articulation of these foundational principles and our pledge to build a legacy that reflects responsible leadership, nurtures future owners from within our ranks, and ensures that [business name] remains a trusted partner and a positive force in this community for generations to come.

Avoid adding lots of detailed key performance indicators (KPIs) or measurement requirements beyond what is already implied (e.g., tracking VTO hours, number of workshops, etc.). Keep measurements simple, at least in the Stewardship Plan language. Focus on guideposts that will help your business move gracefully and professionally into the future and be a great steward in your community.

The point of these suggestions is to deepen the plan's integration and resonance within your business's culture, primarily through reinforcing language and communications that you control, rather than adding operational burdens. Choose the ones that feel most authentic and useful for your specific goals and culture. There is no right or wrong when it comes to drafting a Stewardship Plan, nor even too long or too short. Change it as you wish, even as you are busy changing the world with your small business.

STEWARDSHIP SPOTLIGHT

ICEBUG SWEDISH TRACTION FOOTWEAR (JONSERED, SWEDEN): Icebug was founded in 2001 by a mother-and-son team and remains an independent, privately owned company in a niche market. This small business had the innovative idea to sell shoes equipped with dynamic steel studs, designed to provide superior traction in cold, icy climates where freezing weather (at or below 0°C or 32°F) lasts 60 to 100 days per year. The goal was simple but powerful: to keep feet warm, dry, and, most importantly, upright during treacherous winter months. As it turns out, that was a very good idea.

Icebug demonstrates stewardship to the environment by focusing on durable products, using recycled and bio-based materials where possible, and working continuously to reduce their carbon footprint. They also prioritize the safety and satisfaction of their customers. At their headquarters in Jonsered, Sweden, if someone in customer service has a technical question about a shoe model, they can simply walk a few meters to the person who designed it.

Within their team, Icebug promotes a strong work-life balance and a commitment to outdoor and environmental values. For example, employees regularly join open lunch runs through the forest right outside the office. Icebug also sponsors The Frozen Lake Marathon, one of the coolest winter running experiences anywhere on Earth!

3.2 INTEGRATING PROPER GOVERNANCE PROCEDURES

THINK OF GOVERNANCE PROVISIONS AS the rulebook behind your Stewardship Plan—the specific procedures and structures that help ensure your commitments move beyond good intentions and across more than one generation of ownership if possible. While your Stewardship Plan outlines *what* your business aims to do (such as supporting the community, developing employees for ownership, or protecting the environment), governance provisions explain *how* those commitments will be carried out, monitored, and protected over time. These provisions address practical questions like:

Who is responsible for overseeing the Plan?

How will progress be reviewed and decisions made?

What mechanisms will hold the business accountable?

How will stewardship commitments remain intact through leadership changes or a potential sale?

Governance provisions are the built-in guardrails that move stewardship from a set of values into a system of action.

As noted earlier (Section 1.7), B Corporation certification requires a formal change in a company's legal structure—specifically, its governance—to be accountable to *all* stakeholders, not just shareholders. This change ensures that a business's stakeholder commitments are legally binding on current and future owners, helping protect the integrity of its mission over time. While these changes are voluntary for non–B Corps, adopting similar governance provisions is a wise step for any business serious about stewardship. This is how you embed your values into your company's legal DNA.

Continuing to build on the Riverview Financial Planning's Stewardship Plan that we drafted and subsequently evolved in the preceding section, here are some specific, low-complexity, high-impact governance provisions one could add or integrate to make this sample Stewardship Plan work even more effectively. The newly added governance elements are in **bold type** in the following modified Plan.

[MODIFIED] Stewardship Plan for Riverview Financial Planning, LLC:

Date: March 27, 20__

A) Our Purpose and Commitment. Riverview Financial Planning, LLC is dedicated to providing exceptional financial planning services built on trust, integrity, and a long-term perspective. This Stewardship Plan outlines how we intend to operate responsibly towards our clients, our team, our community, and the future of the firm itself. This plan is integral to our mission and guides our daily decisions and actions.

B) Core Principles. We are committed to upholding the following principles in all aspects of our business:

1. Client Stakeholder Group:

- Fiduciary Duty: Acting solely in the best interests of our clients.

- Transparency: Communicating clearly, honestly, and openly about our services, fees, and recommendations.

- Confidentiality: Protecting client information with the utmost care and security.

- Long-Term Relationships: Building enduring partnerships with clients based on mutual trust and understanding.

- Competence: Maintaining the highest levels of professional knowledge and skill. This firm will support and encourage everyone to obtain the necessary education and credentials to support our clients' needs and goals.

2. Employee Stakeholder Group:

- A Fair and Respectful Workplace: Being a leader in terms of compensation and benefits, fostering a positive and inclusive work environment, and treating every team member with respect.

- Professional Growth: Investing in the ongoing training, development, and credentialing of our team members.

- Work-Life Balance: Supporting the well-being of our employees by encouraging reasonable workloads and flexibility where possible.

- Clear Path for Advancement: Providing opportunities for career growth within the firm.

3. Community Stakeholder Group (focusing on the community of Riverview):

- Ethical Conduct: Operating with integrity and upholding the highest ethical standards in all our interactions within the Riverview community and beyond.

- Focused Local Engagement: We commit to actively engaging with and supporting the Riverview community through focused, consistent efforts that will include:

  o Financial Literacy Initiative: Dedicate firm resources (time and expertise) to improving financial literacy within the Riverview community. We will aim to deliver at least [e.g., two to four] financial wellness workshops annually, partnering with local schools, community centers, or nonprofits serving [e.g., young adults, seniors, or underserved populations—*choose a focus*].

  o Strategic Nonprofit Partnership: Establish and maintain a long-term partnership with at least one specific Riverview-based nonprofit organization whose mission aligns with our firm's values. This partnership will involve [e.g., a combination of financial support, skills-based volunteering using our financial expertise, and/or board service].

  o Supported Employee Volunteerism: Encourage and support employee engagement in Riverview community initiatives by providing [e.g., eight to twelve hours] of paid volunteer time off (VTO) per employee annually, usable for firm-organized events or individual volunteering aligned with our focus areas.

  o Local Sourcing: Prioritize using local Riverview-area suppliers and vendors for office needs, catering, and events whenever practical and economically feasible.

- Responsible Resource Use: Operating our office efficiently to minimize waste and conserve resources. This firm's goal is to become a paperless office within five years.

4. Firm (Business/Entity) Stakeholder Group (Ownership and Succession):

- Continuity of Service: Ensuring the long-term stability and continuity of the firm for the benefit of our clients and employees through proactive succession planning.

- Internal Succession Priority: Prioritizing the development of internal talent for future leadership and ownership roles.

- Defined Ownership Track: Maintaining a clear, merit-based pathway for dedicated employees to achieve partnership and participate in the ownership equity of the firm. This includes mentorship and preparation for leadership responsibilities.

- Financial Prudence: Managing the firm's finances responsibly to ensure its long-term health and viability.

C) Governance, Implementation, and Accountability:

1. Leadership Accountability and Oversight:

- **Designated Stewardship Partner: One partner will be formally designated as the "stewardship partner," holding primary responsibility for overseeing the implementation of this Plan and championing its principles within the firm.**

- **Standing Agenda Item: Stewardship progress, including community engagement activities and ownership track development, will be a standing agenda item for review during regular [e.g., quarterly] partner/leadership meetings.**

2. Role Assignment and Execution:

- **Formal Coordination of Roles: The coordination of roles for specific initiatives (e.g., financial literacy initiative lead, nonprofit partnership liaison, VTO tracking) will be formally assigned to specific individuals (partner, manager, or designated employee) and acknowledged as part of their responsibilities.**

- Decision-Making Authority: Decisions regarding the selection of key stewardship partners (e.g., the primary nonprofit partner) or significant resource allocation for stewardship initiatives require partner approval. Day-to-day coordination decisions rest with the assigned coordinators.

3. Resource Allocation:

- Budget Integration: Anticipated investment and costs associated with stewardship activities (e.g., materials for workshops, potential donations, software for tracking) and allocated time (e.g., VTO budget) will be incorporated into the firm's annual budgeting process.

4. Performance and Development Integration:

- Performance Conversations: Contributions to stewardship goals (e.g., participating in VTO, leading literacy workshops, mentoring colleagues on the ownership track) will be positively acknowledged during annual performance conversations, particularly for those aspiring to leadership or partnership roles.

- Ownership Track Criteria: Progress and engagement related to the firm's overall stewardship values will be considered as part of the qualitative assessment for advancement on the defined ownership track.

5. Monitoring and Review:

- Annual Stewardship Review Meeting: Leadership (partners and relevant coordinators) will conduct a dedicated annual meeting to review progress against this Plan. This review will include:

  o A summary of community engagement activities (workshops delivered, VTO hours used, partnership impact).

  o An update on ownership track progress and mentorship.

  o Feedback from employees and community partners (where applicable).

  o Identification of successes, challenges, and areas for improvement.

- **Actionable Output: The annual review will result in a brief internal summary and affirmed priorities or necessary adjustments to the Plan for the upcoming year.**

6. Communication and Transparency:

- **Internal Communication Protocol: Updates on stewardship initiatives, successes, and upcoming opportunities will be communicated regularly to all team members via [e.g., dedicated time in team meetings, internal email updates].**

- **External Communication (Selective): Key stewardship commitments (like the financial literacy initiative or nonprofit partnership) may be communicated externally via the firm website or client communications where appropriate, reinforcing the firm's values.**

7. Policy Alignment:

- **Periodic Policy Review: Key firm policies (e.g., employee handbook, purchasing guidelines) will be reviewed periodically [e.g., every two to three years] to ensure continuing alignment with this Stewardship Plan.**

D) **Operational Integration. Beyond the specific governance measures set forth in this Plan, these stewardship principles shall be integrated into our daily operations, client service standards, employee policies, and strategic planning processes.**

E)   Conclusion. Our commitment to stewardship ensures that Riverview Financial Planning, LLC not only provides outstanding financial guidance but also operates as a responsible, ethical, and sustainable firm for the long term. We believe this approach benefits our clients, empowers our team, strengthens our community, and secures the future legacy of the firm.

This version maintains the core principles and specific community focus discussed previously while embedding the crucial governance mechanisms needed for effective implementation and accountability within this twelve-person financial planning firm. The sample Stewardship Plan, as it has evolved and been modified immediately above, is applicable to a wide variety of professional service businesses, larger and smaller. By implementing these governance provisions, this small business can create a robust framework for ensuring that its Stewardship Plan is not just a document, but a living, breathing commitment that drives real change within the firm and in the community. The key is to create a system of accountability, transparency, and continuous improvement.

Here is a simple but effective checklist for drafting effective governance provisions in your Stewardship Plan:

Leadership Accountability: Who is ultimately responsible?

Oversight and Monitoring: How is progress tracked and reviewed?

Decision-Making: How are decisions related to the Plan made?

Integration: How is the Plan embedded in existing structures or documents?

Transparency and Communication: How is information shared?

Resource Allocation: How are time and money dedicated?

Enforcement/Consistency: How is adherence encouraged?

Incentives and Rewards: How are those responsible for the Plan acknowledged and rewarded?

When in doubt, start simple and give yourself time to evolve these governance provisions from experience and with the help of your team. These provisions do not need to be complicated, but they do need to be effective. It is your business, so if your governance provisions do not work well, or well enough, fix them and continue your efforts. Perfection is not the goal; making a difference is.

STEWARDSHIP SPOTLIGHT

HARNEY & SONS (MILLERTON, NEW YORK, U.S.) Now in its third generation of family ownership, Harney & Sons began in 1983 when John Harney developed a passion for fine teas. John started blending distinctive tea varieties in his basement, serving them to guests at the inn he operated in Salisbury, Connecticut.

Today, Harney & Sons carries an extensive selection of Fair Trade Certified™ teas, supporting fair trade practices that promote sustainable livelihoods, safe working conditions, environmental protection, and transparent supply chains worldwide. They have also partnered with 1% for the Planet for over a decade, donating 1% of their sales to environmental organizations across the globe—and actively encouraging their business associates to do the same.

The Harney family and their staff are proud to contribute to a global movement focused on protecting the environment, one percent at a time. As of early 2025, with their customers' help, Harney & Sons will have donated over $6 million to environmental causes through 1% for the Planet.

3.3 CRAFTING YOUR LEGACY THROUGH STEWARDSHIP

No one ever says, "My business lasted too long, and it did too well."

In fact, too many small businesses *and* their legacies fail to last even five years. Small business startup failures are the rule, not the exception. To be a good steward to your stakeholders, this has to change. You have to build your business right; that demands strong leadership with a vision. Of course it does—everyone says that in every business building book I have ever read, but that does not make it happen. The tasks of building a business and being a good steward to all of your stakeholders are complementary, but require very different skill sets. Good leaders have to figure out how to do both well, and this section is about such leadership.

Part Two of this book covered how to build a business as a technician. Add to that your own strengths and your own passion and skills, and lead. But do not be afraid to learn and listen, a lot, along the way. Strong leaders are not dictators. If you cannot or will not surround yourself with talent that is, or can be, better than you, you cannot create a legacy. You are building a one-generational business if that. That's direct, but as a small business owner, you need to hear it.

Small business owners who aim to build something lasting for their stakeholders must embrace the mindset that leadership is a temporary role, not a lifetime entitlement. Think custodian, not commander. This is especially true in businesses designed to span generations, where continuity depends less on the original founder and more on a steady flow of new and great talent. A deeper bench is not optional; it is essential. Viewing leadership as a caretaker role shifts the focus from personal control to shared responsibility—fostering humility, accountability, and long-term thinking. It recognizes the business as part of a larger ecosystem of people: team members, customers, and the broader world waiting to be served. That is stewardship.

3.3.1. An example of great leadership. Yvon Chouinard (pronounced ee-von shwee-nard in the U.S.), the founder of Patagonia, offers a compelling example of a leader who embodies good stewardship for all stakeholders—with a special emphasis on the environment. Like many entrepreneurs, Chouinard started small. His first business, Chouinard Equipment, crafted rugged climbing gear from a small blacksmith's shop for a close-knit community of climbers. As demand grew, Chouinard and his team began exploring how to minimize their impact on the environment while growing a sustainable business. This small, hands-on company eventually evolved into Patagonia, a brand now known worldwide—but its heart and habits were shaped in the early days when every decision mattered.

In the early 1970s, while traveling in Scotland, Chouinard purchased several rugby shirts that climbers appreciated for their durability. Their unexpected popularity among customers marked Patagonia's first steps into outdoor apparel. From that humble beginning, the company expanded thoughtfully, creating rugged clothing suited to the extreme conditions of places like the southern Andes and Cape Horn region known as Patagonia.

Recognizing that financial success could fuel deeper purpose, Chouinard worked to make Patagonia an outstanding place to work and a catalyst for environmental activism. By the mid-1980s, Patagonia had opened an on-site cafeteria serving healthy, mostly vegetarian meals and introduced on-site child care—both remarkable examples at the time of internal stewardship. Around 1986, Patagonia formalized its environmental commitment by pledging either 1% of sales or 10% of profits, whichever was greater, to grassroots environmental causes. Patagonia's early journey powerfully demonstrates that with a clear sense of purpose, a small business can grow stronger, last longer, and change the world — one thoughtful decision at a time.

As Patagonia grew, Chouinard remained committed to using the business as a tool for good. That lifelong commitment culminated in 2022, when he and his family made the extraordinary decision to transfer ownership of Patagonia to protect its values and intensify its environmental mission. From a September 2022, Patagonia press release, in Yvon Chouinard's own words:

> *I never wanted to be a businessman. I started as a craftsman, making climbing gear for my friends and myself, then got into apparel. As we began to witness the extent of global warming and ecological destruction, and our own contribution*

to it, Patagonia committed to using our company to change the way business was done. If we could do the right thing while making enough to pay the bills, we could influence customers and other businesses, and maybe change the system along the way.

We started with our products, using materials that caused less harm to the environment. We gave away 1% of sales each year. We became a certified B Corp and a California benefit corporation, writing our values into our corporate charter so they would be preserved. More recently, in 2018, we changed the company's purpose to: We're in business to save our home planet.

While we're doing our best to address the environmental crisis, it's not enough. We needed to find a way to put more money into fighting the crisis while keeping the company's values intact.

One option was to sell Patagonia and donate all the money. But we couldn't be sure a new owner would maintain our values or keep our team of people around the world employed.

Another path was to take the company public. What a disaster that would have been. Even public companies with good intentions are under too much pressure to create short-term gain at the expense of long-term vitality and responsibility.

Truth be told, there were no good options available. So, we created our own.

Instead of "going public," you could say we're "going purpose." Instead of extracting value from nature and transforming it into wealth for investors, we'll use the wealth Patagonia creates to protect the source of all wealth. Here's how it works: 100% of the company's voting stock transfers to the Patagonia Purpose Trust, created to protect the company's values; and 100% of the nonvoting stock has been given to the Holdfast Collective, a nonprofit dedicated to fighting the environmental crisis and defending nature. The funding will come from Patagonia: each year, the money we make after reinvesting in the business will be distributed as a dividend to help fight the crisis.

It's been nearly 50 years since we began our experiment in responsible business, and we are just getting started. If we have any hope of a thriving planet—much less a thriving business—50 years from now, it is going to take all of us doing what we can with the resources we have. This is another way we've found to do our part.

Despite its immensity, the earth's resources are not infinite, and it's clear we've exceeded its limits. But it's also resilient. We can save our planet if we commit to it.

What makes Chouinard's story powerful is not just that he started simple and small, and built a big business. It is that he did it while questioning the system, refusing to compromise on his values, and ultimately giving away the ownership of the company to ensure its profits would go toward his chosen cause–his stated purpose.

Bold choices do not guarantee success. But they invite it. And in stewardship, boldness may be the most underappreciated asset of all.

Patagonia's extraordinary decision may have made headlines, but its real lesson is this: when small businesses grow strong with purpose at their core, they can drive change far beyond what anyone imagines. Stewardship is not just idealism—it is a strategy for lasting, meaningful impact. Do everything you can and influence others to help you—to help us. If one small business can grow, endure, and inspire global change through stewardship, imagine what fifty million can do.

""Fortes fortuna adiuvat."

Terence, 2nd century BCE
(Roman Republic)

3.3.2. The personal connection is what matters. At the start of this book, we talked about the need for small business owners to genuinely care about the stakeholders they serve. Of course, I am preaching to the choir here. You would be hard-pressed to find anyone more motivated than an owner who is figuring out how to survive and meet next month's payroll. Add to that a small business leader who looks into the eyes of a grateful and appreciative stakeholder–an individual who cannot find the words of appreciation for the difference you are making or trying to make in their life. Let's focus on the latter.

Small business owners are leaders who must work closely, and often personally, with all of their stakeholders, including employees, partners, customers, and suppliers. The CEO of a Fortune 500 company+ can delegate these responsibilities; small business leaders have their hands on every aspect of the business for the first ten years or so. And that is your greatest advantage! You not only have to care, you have to demonstrate it and show others how it is done. You lead by example. That is an awesome responsibility and opportunity. It is your secret weapon.

Changing the world, one small community at a time, is how stewardship works best. It is harder, I think, to significantly support a cause, long-term, on the opposite side of the world unless you take the time to visit and see it for yourself, and then monitor the progress they are making with your support. The point is, it is just as hard trying to make a connection from the fortieth floor of a downtown skyscraper when, as CEO, you never directly see or hear from most of your stakeholders. But driving twenty minutes across town to see something for yourself, or welcoming visitors to your office who wish to talk to you in person to share their needs, concerns, and appreciation is something very different.

When customers feel a personal connection to a small business, they are more likely to become your loyal advocates. Similarly, positive relationships with employees can create a supportive and engaging workplace culture, enhancing job satisfaction, productivity, and retention. Employees who feel valued and respected are more likely to be committed to the company's success and uphold its values. The personal touch often inherent in a small business can lead to a stronger sense of shared values and responsibility among owners, employees, and customers, fostering a more ethical and community-oriented approach to business. These close relationships, built on trust and mutual respect, can contribute significantly to a small business's reputation and, ultimately, its long-term success. This is how stewardship builds legacies.

3.3.3. The enabling role of profitability. There is a growing chorus of voices suggesting that businesses in general should minimize or curtail profits to make the world a better place. While well-intended, this perspective often feels, at least to small business owners, somewhere between oversimplified and condescending. And understandably so. It is easy to advocate for lower profits from a distance, especially if you have never had to make payroll, sign a personal guarantee on a lease, or balance the wellbeing of your team with the reality of a tight cash flow. Here is what those critics often miss—perhaps because they have not walked in your shoes:

- Profitability is not the enemy of stewardship. Small business owners, especially in the early stages, often operate with thin margins and strong personal ties to their employees and customers. The idea that profits and people are mutually exclusive simply does not reflect how most small businesses operate.

- It can feel like a moral judgment—as if wanting your business to be sustainable and successful somehow makes you greedy or uncaring, even when you have risked your home and personal savings to bring your vision to life.

- Without profit, there is no business. And without the business, there are no jobs, no customer service, no community involvement, no impact. Profit is not the purpose, but it is the engine.

- It ignores the risks and realities of entrepreneurship. Too often, those advocating this view have never had to run a business themselves. Yet they are quick to prescribe how others should run theirs.

- It is short-sighted for succession and long-term ownership. Future owners—especially next-generation family members or employee-owners—will not invest their time, energy, or money into a business that fails to deliver a competitive return. Stewardship must also account for sustainability.

Profitability does not contradict stewardship, it makes it possible. When used wisely, profits create breathing room, resilience, and the freedom to do right by all stakeholders, not just one.

I will concede that such thinking might be marginally applicable, or at least *thinking material*, when applied to a much larger or publicly traded company (i.e., Fortune 500 company+), but it makes no sense to anyone who has ever run and built a strong, durable, small business. Lead the way, build your legacy, and walk confidently and proudly in the opposite direction. Being a good steward demands it!

Profitability directly enables small businesses to invest in the well-being of their employees through fair wages, comprehensive benefits and wellness programs. Being profitable is part of the foundation of success. To this end, *take the high road* and push back in a positive, enlightened manner. Here are some more nuanced ways to reframe the concept:

- *Balancing Profit and People:* This acknowledges that both are important, and that there is a need for equilibrium.

- *Sustainable Growth, Not at the Expense of People:* This focuses on long-term viability and ethical practices.

- *People-Centered Profitability*: This flips the phrase, emphasizing that valuing people can actually drive profit.

- *Ethical Business Practices:* This is a broader term that encompasses fair treatment of employees, customers, and the community.

- *Community-Focused Business*: This can show that a business is concerned about more than just the bottom line.

Add these phrases to your marketing materials and change attitudes even as you change the world!

STEWARDSHIP SPOTLIGHT

OUTLAND DENIM (TAMBORINE MOUNTAIN, QUEENSLAND, AUSTRALIA–WITH PRODUCTION IN KAMPONG CHAM AND PHNOM PENH, CAMBODIA): Founded by James Bartle in 2016, Outland Denim is a small business producing high-quality denim clothing while upholding revolutionary social and environmental standards. Outland offers a full range of styles for men and women—including jeans, shorts, jackets, and other denim-based apparel—all crafted with sustainability and ethics at their core.

In their own words: "We are about #DenimForFreedom. We have a unique business model designed to create a cycle of empowerment for those in need. We provide opportunity and a safe and supportive working environment, a living wage, training, health care, and education to people who have experienced or are at risk of experiencing modern slavery, exploitation, or abuse. Outland Denim is so much more than a denim company."

Outland Denim's role in changing the world is realized through life-changing employment opportunities for survivors of exploitation, contributing directly to their healing and reintegration into society. Their production facilities in Cambodia are built specifically to achieve this social mission, hiring, paying, and treating employees with dignity, fairness, and long-term support.

3.4 MEASURING AND REPORTING YOUR STEWARDSHIP IMPACT

ONE OF THE JOYS OF self-publishing is that I can and will update this book at least annually, and this section in particular. As we all learn more together about deploying good stewardship through a small business and you share some of your stories and successes with me via my website (www.DavidGrauSr.com), I will add them to our collective knowledge base. You can learn more about how others choose to measure and report on their stewardship impact through my blog posts, and your fellow small business owners around the world who buy this book next year can learn from your successes. In the meantime, here is what I think:

a) **Show the world what you are doing–and why it matters.** In the due diligence that I did searching for small businesses that are and have been good stewards of all their stakeholders, many had no information on their websites about what they did. Stewardship doesn't need a spotlight for ego's sake; visibility has a purpose: it normalizes doing good. It leads others. It earns trust. Create a dedicated page (e.g., "Our Impact," "Sustainability," "Community Commitment," "Changing the World Together"). Tell your community, your current and future customers and employees what you are doing—and why it matters.

Websites, newsletters, even press releases can be used to share your story. Write or outline an article for your local newspaper or publish your results through your local Chamber of Commerce or trade association. Talk to your neighboring small business owners and look for ways to work together on a common cause. Just don't be quiet.

b) **Focus on real stories, not just real numbers.** Measurement is essential, but stories give your efforts heart. Why did you support that local nonprofit? What happened when your team volunteered its time and efforts? What feedback did a supplier give you after you made an important change? What do you know about stewardship that other small businesses probably don't?

Use numbers to show scale—hours volunteered, dollars donated, emissions reduced—but always pair them with human moments. And if something didn't work as planned? Say so. Report with honesty, not perfection. The world doesn't need polished. It needs real.

c) **Use your Stewardship Plan as a guide.** In Section 3.1, we worked through a detailed example of a Stewardship Plan. Built into the sample draft is a section that addresses implementation and accountability. This is a great starting point for developing your own measuring and reporting requirements.

In Section 3.2, we upgraded the basic plan to include an enhanced *Governance, Implementation, and Accountability* section. Assign responsibilities. Set expectations. Reflect annually. Get specific about what measurements and reporting you expect as an owner. Include a communications provision for both internal use and external use. With each passing year, gradually evolve your Stewardship Plan in all these areas. Experience is the best teacher.

d) **Keep it simple and relevant.** You don't need a 40-page glossy impact report. But you do need to care—and to show others that you do through your actions. Start with what you already track or know:

- **Environmental**: Energy and water usage, waste diversion, sustainable materials, recycling
- **Social**: Employee well-being, community partnerships, local sourcing
- **Governance**: Ethical practices, diversity of decision-makers, transparency
- **Economic**: Fair wages, shared ownership through a succession plan, profit reinvestment

Make reporting meaningful, not burdensome. And tailor it to what is most relevant in your sector and community.

e) **Global change starts with local action.** There are more than 500 million small businesses worldwide. Most have 20 or fewer people. Imagine if even a small percentage of them integrated stewardship into their operations and shared their efforts publicly. The ripple effects—on trust, employment, supply chains, and local environments—would be immense.

When you report your stewardship efforts, you're not just documenting what you did. You're building momentum for a global shift in what it means to run a business well.

f) **Contribute to our Gallery of Good Stewards.** This book features 25 Stewardship Spotlights, but there are many, many more stories to tell. Nominate your own business, or one that you admire, to the growing online gallery (there is no cost or obligation) at:

https://davidgrausr.com/stewardship-gallery

These small businesses and others like them, perhaps yours, are the real heroes of this story. This is more than recognition—it is an invitation to show others that change is possible, even for the smallest businesses.

Finally, here are some basic but key principles for small businesses in terms of measuring and reporting your stewardship impact:

- **Start small:** Pick two to three key areas most relevant to your business and stakeholders.

- **Be consistent:** Track metrics regularly (e.g., monthly, quarterly), over the course of time, to see trends.

- **Use what you already have:** Leverage information you already collect (utility bills, payroll, invoices, volunteer logs, surveys, etc.).

- **Invite others:** Employees, customers, and suppliers often want to help support a worthy cause.

- **Celebrate progress, not perfection:** Continuous improvement is the goal.

Measuring and sharing your impact isn't just good practice. It is an act of leadership. It shows your team and your community that your values show up in your decisions and actions. It creates accountability. And it fosters resilience by aligning your business with something bigger and greater.

Changing the world isn't a slogan. It's a daily practice. And measurement is how we make sure the practice is real.

STEWARDSHIP SPOTLIGHT

AVANI ECO (DENPASAR, INDONESIA): From Bali to the world! This small business was established in 2014 to provide a full range of sustainable packaging and hospitality products made from renewable and natural ingredients. Strongly rooted in the principles of "reduce, reuse, and recycle," Avani adds "responsibility" to that list as a core value across its business practices.

Avani has developed groundbreaking technology that replaces disposable plastic products—which can take hundreds or even thousands of years to decompose—with renewable, plant-based alternatives. Their products, made from cassava starch and other sustainable materials, are fully biodegradable and compostable. By hiring local people in Indonesia and sourcing materials from regional farmers, Avani not only creates environmentally friendly alternatives to harmful plastics, it also supports the local economy. In terms of stewardship, Avani Eco:

- Provides employment opportunities in a growing green industry

- Offers environmentally friendly alternatives to single-use plastics

- Sources sustainable plant-based materials locally

- Directly addresses the global plastic pollution crisis

- Promotes environmental awareness and sustainable practices within Indonesia

Avani's mission is to protect Mother Earth by choosing sustainable products that make a real difference. No more plastic for a better future.

3.5 THE COLD, HARD BUSINESS CASE

ONE OF THE MOST IMPORTANT and memorable exercises in my first year of law school was to argue the same case in front of a jury of my peers, twice; once as plaintiff's counsel, and once as defense counsel. I remember the event and the lessons learned now thirty years later. And to complete this section's title, this is The Cold, Hard Business Case *Against Stewardship*.

Throughout this book, I have written as Dr. Jekyll—the thoughtful, values-driven small business owner who believes that stewardship is not only possible but essential. But in this section, I will take a sharp and deliberate turn. Call it my *Mr. Hyde moment*. Thank you, Robert Louis Stevenson for the stage. For the next few pages, I will shed the voice of the good steward and speak plainly as the hard-nosed, unsentimental capitalist—the kind who sees stewardship not as noble, but naïve. Why? Because to fully understand the value of stewardship, you must first hear—and grapple with—the cold, hard business case against it. Only by giving Mr. Hyde his say can we fully appreciate why Dr. Jekyll's path matters.

In the most calculating view, stewardship is a self-imposed handicap in a world where business is a fight for survival. A smart and shrewd owner (is there any better kind?) sees stakeholders—employees, customers, suppliers, even the community— not as partners to nurture but as tools to be leveraged. Sentimentality is a liability; efficiency is an asset. If the business fails, even as the owner loses their home or files for bankruptcy, stakeholders will quickly move on to the next provider without a second thought.

> *"Collectivism holds that the individual has no rights, that his life and work belong to the group...and that the group may sacrifice him at its own whim to its own interests."*
>
> Ayn Rand, *Textbook of Americanism*
> *(1946)*

Stewardship, critics correctly argue, often devolves into *performative altruism*—a branding tactic rather than a business strategy. Optics are everything. A donation here, a greenwashed statement there, and the public is more than satisfied, while real focus remains on maximizing profit for those who took the risk of ownership. In this model, reputation is currency to be spent, not preserved. And if stakeholders don't like it? They're free to leave—only to find that most successful competitors operate the same way. If they didn't, they wouldn't survive either.

Small business is a high-risk endeavor. If it collapses, the unsentimental owner walks away—wealthier, wiser, or simply ready to retire. From this perspective, stewardship is a fool's errand: a drag on personal enrichment in service of people who owe the owner nothing. Customers chasing discounts will leave anyway, and short-term gains reward the ruthless, not the generous. In the eyes of a pure opportunist, stewardship isn't good business—it's unnecessary charity, best kept out of the workplace and reserved for personal life. Besides, business owners pay city, county, state and federal taxes to address all these causes, anyway.

By focusing solely on profitability and extracting maximum value from every stakeholder interaction—as competitors do—owners may achieve faster financial gain, easier exits, and lower overhead. That, after all, is the job. In cutthroat industries, this kind of efficiency can even create an important edge over more conscientious competitors burdened by higher ethical and operational standards. Would you rather invest in a business that wants to save the environment, or one that is focused on delivering a great product at the lowest possible price? Taking one's eye off the business to support a cause is a mistake most small business owners make only once.

In the short term, the costs of poor stewardship are rarely noticeable and easily explained away:

- "We're just a small business trying to get by."

- "We'll help when we can—we have to make payroll."

- "We're doing our best to keep our prices down and our service excellent."

That was your strongest competitor speaking. Meanwhile, most customers prioritize price and convenience over ethics. Suppliers tolerate mistreatment if the volume is good. Employees, fearing job loss, will accept less than optimum conditions without complaint in exchange for a steady paycheck and some benefits. In this light, stewardship isn't a strategic advantage—it's a voluntary burden. A luxury. An indulgence for owners with the time and money to chase ideals.

Critics of corporate stewardship rightly argue that giving without thought can actually do more harm than good. Businesses are built for profit, not charity. The market rewards outcomes, not good intentions—and stewardship rarely shows up as a win on a profit-and-loss statement. Peter Buffett, son of Warren Buffett, wrote in his 2013 *New York Times* op-ed, *The Charitable-Industrial Complex*: "Philanthropy has become the 'conscience laundering' for those accumulating wealth through questionable means."

His point: giving can become a way to ease guilt rather than address root causes. Anand Giridharadas makes a similar case in *Winners Take All* (2018), arguing that the elite often try to "change the world" in ways that preserve their own privilege. Even companies like Bombas—featured earlier in this book as an example of great stewardship—have been fairly criticized for their approach. The buy-one/donate-one model is properly challenged for a host of reasons:

- It treats symptoms, not causes.

- Free goods won't fix poverty or homelessness.

- Feel good giving makes people feel involved, and then they disengage.

- It fosters dependency, not empowerment.

- Stewardship often becomes marketing with little real impact.

- It lets companies collect praise and profits while offloading the hard work to others.

- In developing countries, it can undermine local producers and disrupt fragile economies.

Rutger Bregman, in *Utopia for Realists* (2016), argues that real change comes from empowerment, not giveaways. Michael Hobbes echoes this in his 2017 article, *Stop Trying to Save the World*, highlighting how many well-meaning aid programs provide temporary relief—and lasting harm. And the list goes on…

At some point, this begins to feel like *heads you win, tails I lose*. If there's no clear impact—and the risks of unintended harm are real—then I'll just keep my earnings and do the occasional personal good deed instead.

And that, in a nutshell, is the case against stewardship. I'm an author, not a judge. I could write an entire book defending that cold-hearted view. The truth is, as a small business owner, you don't *have* to be a good steward. You're not a bad person if you just want to run your business and take care of your own.

But to those who say stewardship isn't about handouts—that it's about addressing the conditions that made them necessary—I say: you're absolutely right. Not all giving is good giving, as to the recipient at least. Real stewardship doesn't create illusions of progress. It demands thoughtful action, long-term commitment, and often, quiet work that never makes it into a marketing campaign. It's not performative; it's purposeful.

And for the record—if someone is hungry and cold, calling basic compassion a "freebie" sounds crass. Do what you can, when you can, for whom you can. There *are* two sides to most stories, this one included. But this isn't moot court. Real lives are at stake. And too many of our fellow humans are suffering.

**"A wise man gets more use
from his enemies than a fool from his friends."**

Baltasar Gracián
(Spain)

Small business owners can't change entire systems alone. But they can question, vote, lead, and show policymakers what genuine impact looks like—face-to-face, one stakeholder at a time. Holding the line until help arrives is not a wasted effort. When millions of small businesses act with purpose, systemic change becomes possible.

But stewardship takes some work. You have to want it. Dr. Jekyll and Mr. Hyde, importantly, are the same person (the *Strange Case of Dr. Jekyll and Mr. Hyde* (1886)). This story reflects the dual nature within all of us: good and evil, generosity and greed, stewardship and self-interest. The choice between cold efficiency and real stewardship shapes more than your business–it shapes your community, your values, and the future surrounding your family. And it shapes *you* as a business owner and leader, and as a human being.

STEWARDSHIP SPOTLIGHT

SOMEONE SOMEWHERE (MEXICO CITY, MEXICO): This small business was founded to empower Indigenous artisans across Mexico by combining ancient craftsmanship with modern apparel and accessories. Based in Mexico City, the company partners with hundreds of rural artisans—most of them women—offering fair wages, sustainable employment, and a global platform for their work.

Their products, ranging from backpacks to jackets to lifestyle accessories, blend traditional hand embroidery and weaving techniques with contemporary designs. Each product is signed by the artisan who helped create it, building a personal connection between maker and customer. Someone Somewhere's mission goes beyond commerce: they are dedicated to preserving cultural traditions, promoting sustainability through natural materials and low-impact production, and providing economic opportunities in some of Mexico's most marginalized regions.

Through thoughtful stewardship, Someone Somewhere proves that small businesses can create profound change—one artisan, one community, and one story at a time.

3.6 STAKEHOLDER-BY-STAKEHOLDER ACTION GUIDE

STEWARDSHIP LIVES IN ACTION—NOT IN marketing slogans, not in theory, and not in one-time good deeds. This final section is about taking what you have learned and putting it into motion, stakeholder-by-stakeholder, as you see fit. It is not a checklist. It is a wellspring of ideas—real-world ways to make your values visible through the everyday operations of your business.

If you are thinking about something more magnanimous, please read or re-read the twenty-five (25) *Stewardship Spotlights* throughout this book for inspiration as to what is possible. It is incredible what small business owners are capable of doing!

The action items and ideas are presented in the order of the common stakeholders, or stakeholder groups we've listed and worked with throughout this book, starting with the external stakeholders:

EXTERNAL STAKEHOLDERS

- Customers
- Suppliers
- Community
- Environment

INTERNAL STAKEHOLDERS

- Business/Entity Structure
- Employees
- Owners/Shareholders
- Managers/Officers

Figure 10

Some ideas may spark immediate action. Others may plant seeds for the future, when you are ready. You don't need to do everything—you only need to begin. Start where you are. Use what you have. Change what you can.

CUSTOMERS

These are the people who place their trust in your products or services, your promises, and your purpose. Stewardship here means honoring that trust—with quality, transparency, and care.

Listening & Transparency:

- Meet with ten of your clients every year to share your Stewardship Plans and gather feedback. And then, just listen, listen, listen.

- Identify social or environmental challenges important to your customers and align them with your Stewardship Plan.

- Be honest about pricing, policies, and changes—even when it's inconvenient.

- Respect customer privacy and never sell or share data. Explain clearly how you use information.

Service & Support:

- Provide high-quality customer support and empower employees to solve problems immediately.

- Use social media and surveys to gather feedback, implement changes, and inform customers when you do.

- Develop ethical products and/or services that improve customers' lives—don't cut corners.

- Build relationships through personalized gestures like thank-you notes and milestone gifts.

- Provide free educational resources to help customers use your products and/or services effectively.

- Host an annual client appreciation event and share your stewardship initiatives.

Loyalty & Education:

- Share your Stewardship Plan openly and encourage other business owners to create one.

- Offer transparent pricing with flexible options to reduce financial strain.

- Launch a 'Customer Advisory Board' to get early feedback and ideas for innovation.

- Consider becoming a Certified B Corporation and share that journey with your customers.

- Consider working with 1% for the Planet, a global network. Collective action makes a difference.

- Create local jobs and let customers help you recruit talent from the community.

- Offer internships and apprenticeships, including through customer referrals.

- Share free templates, checklists, or articles with clients if you offer professional services.

SUPPLIERS & SUPPLY CHAIN

Your supply chain is an extension of your values. Treat suppliers like partners, not vendors, and expect the same in return. That is how stewardship travels upstream.

Ethical Sourcing & Accountability:

- Perform annual due diligence on your key suppliers and share your Stewardship Plan, goals, and concerns with them.

- Develop and share a *Supplier Code of Conduct* outlining fair labor, safety, sustainability, and transparency expectations.

- Source supplies from local small businesses when possible and share your stewardship values with them.

- Use industry groups to vet suppliers and align their practices with your values.

Partnership & Communication:

- Engage suppliers in stewardship conversations and support them in developing aligned practices.

- Evaluate supplier alignment with your company values and willingness to improve together.

- Use public platforms to advocate for important causes that your suppliers can see and join.

- Pay suppliers on or before the agreed date and be transparent when changes arise.

- Communicate clearly and consistently with suppliers, keeping them informed of changes.

- Share relevant business plans so suppliers can prepare and contribute insights.

- Be honest about your order volume and avoid over-promising.

Payment & Reliability:

- Refer good suppliers and publicly recognize them for exceptional work.

- Collaborate with suppliers on sustainable practices and share those efforts with customers.

- Respect every member of your suppliers' teams, including delivery drivers and support staff.

- Support suppliers during hardships with flexibility, early payments, or referrals.

COMMUNITY

You're not just located in your community—you are part of it every day. Stewardship means showing up, pitching in, and sharing your success in ways that strengthen the whole.

Hiring & Inclusion:

- Teach stewardship principles to other local business owners by example and discussion. Be a leader.

- Hire locally and offer roles to students, retirees, or those re-entering the workforce whenever possible.

- Use local service providers for business needs to support the local economy.

Space & Events:

- Offer your space to community groups for free or at reduced cost in support of local events.

- Host community skill-sharing workshops in partnership with other businesses.

- Sponsor and volunteer for youth programs and local school initiatives.

- Serve as an emergency support site during local crises when possible.

- Showcase local artists and participate in cultural events to support local heritage.

Advocacy & Service:

- Support civic initiatives like better infrastructure or schools through advocacy.

- Collaborate with other small businesses on focused stewardship initiatives

- Ensure your efforts are inclusive of *all* community members.

- Design operations to minimize disruption to the neighborhood.

- Form a Community Advisory Group to gather local insights and needs.

- Create a *Local Community Focus* section in your Stewardship Plan.

- Offer pro bono services and goods to local nonprofit organizations.

- Invest in beautifying or improving your physical space for public benefit.

- Donate time, money, or goods to local causes and participate in fundraisers.

- Attend and participate in local government meetings and discussions; listen carefully.

- Create products or services that directly benefit charitable causes.

- Support employee volunteerism with paid time off and coordinated opportunities.

- Mentor local youth or entrepreneurs and share knowledge and networks.

- Provide community information and resources relevant to your neighbors.

- Ensure your business is a welcoming, inclusive space for all.

ENVIRONMENT

Good stewards do not just take less—they give back more. Sustainability is about reducing harm, restoring systems, and redesigning how you do business for the long term with a watchful eye on the one planet we all share.

Energy & Emissions:

- Switch to renewable energy providers or purchase renewable energy credits.

- Track and reduce your carbon footprint through small annual goals.

- Encourage eco-friendly commuting among employees with incentives or recognition.

- Adopt a paperless-first policy and minimize unnecessary printing.

- Walk or bike to work if possible and encourage others to do the same.

Waste Reduction:

- Use compostable, recycled, or reusable packaging to reduce waste.

- Print using plant-based inks when possible.

- Furnish your office with secondhand or sustainably sourced items; add live plants to the decor.

- Install water-saving fixtures and create water-conscious staff practices.

- Host or attend sustainable events with minimal disposable materials.

Eco-Friendly Culture:

- Use green banking institutions that avoid funding fossil fuel industries.

- Offer micro-grants to support local environmental initiatives.

- Organize or join community cleanups and greening projects.

- Run an employee 'Green Month' challenge and reward eco-friendly behavior.

- Include an environmental pledge in your Stewardship Plan.

- Reduce business travel by using virtual meetings where possible.

- Source local produce and reduce food waste creatively if in the food industry.

- Conduct an energy audit and invest in energy-efficient solutions.

- Turn off unused equipment and address phantom energy use.

- Work with suppliers to improve their sustainability practices.

- Stay informed on environmental issues and share your sustainability practices with your audience.

BUSINESS/ENTITY STRUCTURE

Stewardship includes protecting and strengthening the very structure of your business—its legal foundation, its financial health, and its long-term durability. This is how you ensure the mission outlives you.

Governance & Agreements:

- Choose the right entity structure (LLC, Corporation, etc.) to match your goals and to support a multi-owner, multi-generational business.

- Professionally document all key agreements and share them with all relevant parties; review and update regularly.

- Use the Three-Bucket Cash Flow System to manage cash flows and improve profitability.

- Regularly determine your business's value through formal or informal appraisals.

- Keep personal and business finances completely separate.

- Establish formal and fair owner compensation structures to support growth and profitability.

Financial Discipline:

- Reinvest profits in sustainable growth and innovation.

- Work with a professional and experienced accountant.

- Protect your brand with appropriate intellectual property filings.

- Develop and follow clear internal governance policies.

- Ensure full legal compliance with expert support as needed.

- Carry appropriate levels of insurance, personally and for your business, and review coverage regularly.

Continuity & Succession Planning:

- Create a succession and contingency plan for leadership and ownership continuity. Read *Building With the End in Mind* to structure a long-term plan to support your stewardship initiatives. Maintain strong financial health through debt management and building up your reserves.

- Make decisions that enhance reputation and long-term ethical standing.

- Build trusted relationships with financial and strategic advisors.

- Align your daily operations with your stated purpose and values.

- Routinely evaluate and manage operational and strategic risks.

- Promote a culture of innovation and adaptability within the business.

EMPLOYEES

These are the people who help build your business every day. Stewardship means helping them thrive—not just survive. Help all of your internal stakeholders become better at what they do; what helps them helps you.

Compensation & Benefits:

- Pay fair, competitive wages that reflect employees' contributions.

- Offer benefits like healthcare, retirement plans, and paid time off if possible.

- Create a safe, inclusive, and respectful workplace.

- Foster a company culture that provides meaning beyond a paycheck.

Culture & Communication:

- Sit down and meet regularly, and listen carefully.

- Implement mentorship programs and pathways for growth.

- Invest in professional development and training tied to advancement.

- Communicate openly and regularly about company updates and challenges.

- Celebrate contributions through recognition programs and personal acknowledgments.

- Support work-life balance and respect personal boundaries.

- Involve employees in meaningful decision-making processes.

- Tie everyday work to your company's broader mission and purpose.

- Handle conflict fairly and compassionately, with focus on resolution.

Growth & Recognition:

- Ensure equity and inclusion in policies, hiring, and culture.

- Protect employee privacy and handle sensitive information responsibly.

- Provide stability during transitions and treat layoffs humanely.

- Celebrate life milestones like birthdays and anniversaries.

- Hold development check-ins regularly, not just annually.

- Encourage cross-functional projects and job rotations.

- Prioritize mental health through EAPs (an Employee Assistance Program), open dialogue, and awareness programs.

- Permit mental health days and host wellness workshops or mindfulness training.

OWNERS/SHAREHOLDERS

Stewardship of ownership means making decisions that support the health of the business, not just the wealth of the owners. That means clarity, respect, alignment, and planning ahead. It also means making equity available to those who earn the opportunity and are willing to buy in.

Alignment & Agreements:

- Create and review clear, professionally drafted ownership agreements annually.

- Align on the business's purpose and values, and revisit regularly as a team.

- Hold regular owner meetings and communicate openly about business performance and goals, successes and shortcomings.

- Recognize all forms of ownership contributions—capital, time, effort, and expertise.

- Separate management and ownership roles to reduce confusion and promote fairness.

- Prioritize long-term business health over short-term personal gain.

Communication & Conflict:

- Respect ownership rights, especially for minority shareholders or silent partners.

- Establish a conflict-resolution process before issues arise.

- Foster mutual respect and assume good intentions during disagreements.

- Keep friendships and family relationships separate from business decisions.

- Create clear policies for ownership transition and exit strategies.

Transitions & Next Generation Ownership:

- Use fair, informed, and objective valuation methods for equity buyouts or succession planning.

- Educate all owners on financials, legal duties, and business trends.

- Support continued education and development for all owners.

- Celebrate shared successes and ownership milestones together.

- Join peer groups or study circles to grow as owners and stewards.

- Introduce ownership tracks to key employees as part of succession planning.

- Benchmark performance against similar businesses for insight, improvement, and accountability.

- Maintain formal financial statements and review them regularly.

- Hire coaches and/or find mentors to support business and leadership development.

- Document annual ownership goals and review them at year-end.

- Update business appraisals at least every five years and adjust plans accordingly.

- Use gradual, small (5%, 10%, etc.) equity sales to bring in and develop next-generation owners.

- Be open to hiring owners' children or relatives with clear expectations.

- Define "active ownership" and require full-time participation in the business as appropriate.

MANAGERS/OFFICERS

Leadership is where culture takes shape. Steward your leaders with support, trust, and vision—because how they lead will shape how your entire business stewards others.

Leadership Development:

- Clearly define leadership roles/duties, authority, and responsibilities in writing.

- Invest in leadership training on strategy, delegation, and emotional intelligence.

- Empower managers to make decisions and lead initiatives with autonomy.

- Regularly communicate the business's big-picture goals and strategic vision.

Empowerment & Accountability:

- Provide the tools, people, and budgets managers need to succeed.

- Create space for honest, constructive feedback without fear of backlash.

- Monitor workloads and avoid overloading key leaders with unrealistic expectations.

- Recognize manager achievements publicly and privately.

- Help managers pursue their own leadership aspirations with support and mentorship.

- Conduct regular performance reviews that emphasize learning and growth.

- Model the behaviors you expect—integrity, humility, resilience, and care.

Strategic Participation:

- Encourage collaboration across departments and unify leadership teams.

- Include managers in strategic planning when possible.

- Celebrate organizational wins with leaders, not just owners.

- Support your managers during periods of major change or uncertainty.

- Allow room for experimentation and small-scale risk-taking within the business.

You've reached the last page of this book—but your journey as a steward is just beginning. Let it begin with one small, intentional step. Then another. Walk forward with purpose, with courage, and in service of something greater than yourself.

Stewardship isn't a to-do list to be completed and thrown aside—it's a way of running your business with conviction every single day. It's about making decisions with the future in mind. It is showing your employees, your customers, your community, and your successors what real responsibility looks like.

And it is time to get things done. So choose one idea. Then choose another. Let your Stewardship Plan evolve as you grow. And remember—millions of small business owners doing the right thing, in their own corners of the world, is how the world changes. Thank you for being one of them.

THE END

...and the beginning!

If you enjoyed this book and the message resonates with you, please share a copy with your nearest small business neighbors and let's start making some waves!

REFERENCES/PART THREE
(IN ALPHABETICAL ORDER):

Avani Eco. 2025. *Our Mission and Sustainable Products.* Avani Eco Official Website. Accessed May 13, 2025. https://www.avanieco.com.

Bastiat, Frédéric. *The State* (L'État), 1848. Reprinted in *Selected Essays on Political Economy*. France.

Bregman, Rutger. 2017. *Utopia for Realists: How We Can Build the Ideal World.* Translated by Elizabeth Manton and Erica Moore. New York: Little, Brown and Company.

Buffett, Peter. 2013. "The Charitable-Industrial Complex." *New York Times*, July 26, 2013. https://www.nytimes.com/2013/07/27/opinion/the-charitable-industrial-complex.html.

Chouinard, Yvon. 2016. *Let My People Go Surfing: The Education of a Reluctant Businessman.* New York: Penguin Books.

Chouinard, Yvon. 2022. "Earth Is Now Our Only Shareholder." *Patagonia.* September 14, 2022. https://www.patagonia.com/ownership/.

Giridharadas, Anand. 2018. *Winners Take All: The Elite Charade of Changing the World.* New York: Alfred A. Knopf.

Harney & Sons. 2025. *Our Commitment to Fair Trade and Sustainability.* Harney & Sons Official Website. Accessed May 13, 2025. https://www.harney.com/pages/our-sustainability.

Hobbes, Michael. 2017. "Stop Trying to Save the World." *HuffPost*, January 19, 2017. https://www.huffpost.com/entry/global-aid-problems_n_587f5dc6e4b0c147f0bcf6c4.

Icebug. 2025. *Our Story: Traction and Sustainability.* Icebug Official Website. Accessed May 13, 2025. https://icebug.com/se/info/about.

Le Slip Français. 2025. *Our Commitments and Ecosystem.* Le Slip Francais Official Website. Accessed May 13, 2025. https://www.leslipfrancais.com/en/pages/commitments.

Outland Denim. 2025. *Denim For Freedom: Our Story.* Outland Denim Official Website. Accessed May 13, 2025. https://www.outlanddenim.com.au/pages/our-story.

Patagonia. 2025. "Company History." Accessed May 14, 2025. https://www.patagonia.com/company-history/.

Rand, Ayn. *Textbook of Americanism*. Originally published in *The Vigil*, 1946. Reprinted in various collections, including *Philosophy: Who Needs It* and *The Ayn Rand Column*.

Someone Somewhere. 2025. *Empowering Artisans through Sustainable Fashion.* Someone Somewhere Official Website. Accessed May 13, 2025. https://www.someonesomewhere.com/pages/about.

ABOUT THE AUTHOR

DAVID GRAU SR., JD, IS schooled in the law, securities regulation, business taxation, entity design and structure, succession planning, and business building. He started small and built and learned, like many other business owners around the world.

In the beginning, David Sr. was a sole proprietor who founded his own securities law practice–a force of one, hanging out his own shingle. While initially enjoying the life of a sole proprietor, he came to grudgingly admit that he *owned a job* rather than a business. So he learned how to fix that and set out to help thousands of others do the same on a national scale.

Subsequently, he was the founding owner of a professional services business that grew from two employee to sixty-five owners/employees, complete with a multimillion dollar annual payroll, a marketing team and a sales team, a full-time bookkeeping staff, and so on. This business focused on financial professionals and specialized in succession, exit, and continuity planning, and business valuation, an operation that provided over 15,000 valuations by the time he *kind of retired*. This is what he knows. Eventually, he completed his own succession plan, selling his equity incrementally back to the business he started and to the next generation owners, all of whom he hired directly or indirectly. And then that business continued on without him, and that completed the circle...up to that point.

Freed from the responsibilities of running a demanding and growing business, he followed his heart and became a full-time author and thinker, and owner of an equestrian property! This book, *The Stewardship Advantage,* is his fifth (and most challenging) published non-fiction work.

David Sr. has previously published four other books on related or supporting subject matter. In 2014, he wrote his first book, *Succession Planning for Financial Advisors/ Building an Enduring Business*, published by Wiley & Sons/Wiley Finance Series. In 2016, he wrote a companion book titled *Buying, Selling and Valuing Financial Practices*, also published by Wiley & Sons. In 2024, he wrote and published his third book, *Building With the End in Mind*, and in 2025, his fourth book and the second in this modern succession planning series, *Acquiring Your Future Through a Succession Plan*. Prior to authoring these books, he wrote a monthly column in *Financial Planning Magazine* for six years on the subjects of succession planning, business perpetuation, equity-management, and valuation. He has written and published two dozen professional white papers, won a host of awards, graced a magazine cover or two, and been the subject of numerous articles for his contributions and thought leadership in the financial services industry.

INDEX

Symbols

1% for the Planet 58, 79, 147, 166

A

Acquiring Your Future Through a Succession Plan vii, 51, 69, 124, 126, 180

Artificial Intelligence 39

Avani Eco 158, 177

B

Basket No. 1 88, 89, 90, 96, 100, 101, 105

Basket No. 2 88, 89, 96, 97, 100, 101, 102, 103, 105, 107

Basket No. 3 88, 89, 90, 93, 96, 97, 102, 103, 105, 111

Bastiat 177

B Corporations 53, 64

B Corps 52, 53, 54, 55, 56, 57, 140

Biolite 125, 126

B Lab 53, 54, 55, 57, 64

Board of Directors 26

Bombas 18, 19, 34, 64, 161

Bregman 161, 177

Buffett 161, 177

Building with the End in Mind vii, 51, 69, 124, 126, 171, 180

Burberry Foundation 64

Bureau of Labor Statistics (BLS) 40, 65

Business/Entity 25, 26, 28, 50, 62, 131, 136, 143, 170

Buy-Sell Agreement 123

C

CAGR 115, 116, 119

Capital Assets 78, 80, 81, 82, 85, 88, 90

C corporation 51, 72, 74, 75, 76, 78

Census Bureau 40, 65

Chouinard 149, 151, 177

Coca-Cola Company 65

Compound Annual Growth Rate 115

Continuity Plan 123

Cost of Goods Sold 91

D

Disregarded entity 74, 105

Dr. Bronner's Magic Soaps 63

E

EBITDA 112

ECOALF 23, 24, 29, 64

Ecoflow 45, 64

Elvis & Kresse 47, 64

Environment 16, 25, 26, 27, 29, 35, 36, 48, 49, 52, 54, 79, 131, 134, 139, 140, 141, 147, 149, 150, 154, 160, 169

Equity 27, 30, 31, 35, 43, 44, 47, 50, 51, 62, 68, 69, 71, 72, 73, 75, 76, 80, 82, 84, 85, 86, 90, 96, 97, 100, 101, 102, 103, 105, 106, 107, 109, 110, 111, 112, 113, 116, 122, 123, 124, 132, 136, 143, 172, 173, 174, 179, 180

Equity-centric 69

Equity Income 105, 106, 112, 113

External stakeholders 25, 27, 28, 29, 31, 33, 35, 61, 69, 164

F

Fair for Life 53, 63

Fair Market Value (FMV) 86, 123

Fair Trade Certification 37

Fair Trade Federation 53, 64, 83

Fortune 500 23, 41, 49, 151, 153

Fortune 500 companies+ 49

Founder's Treadmill 43

FTF (Fair Trade Federation) 64

G

G1 100, 121, 122, 123, 124

G2 100, 101, 107, 121, 122, 123

Gallery of Good Stewards 157

GBCI (Green Business Certification 64

Giridharadas 161, 177

Governance provisions 36, 48,
51, 140, 141, 145, 146

GPM 91, 92, 93, 115

Green Business Certification 53, 64

Greenwashing 56

GRM 110

Gross Profit Margin 91, 92, 115

Gross revenue multiple 110

H

Harney & Sons 146, 147, 177

Hobbes 161, 177

I

Icebug 138, 139, 177

Icebug Swedish Traction Footwear 138

Integrated stewardship 33, 34, 156

Integrated Wealth Planning 87, 126

Intellectual Property 80, 171

Internal Revenue Service 65, 75

Internal stakeholders 25, 26, 27, 28, 29, 30,
31, 35, 62, 67, 69, 84, 86, 97, 98, 103, 172

International Federation of Accountants 40, 64

K

Keepcup 57, 58, 64

Key Performance Indicators (KPI's) 138

King Arthur Baking Company 13, 14, 64

L

Laude The Label 82, 83, 126

Le Slip Français 177

Limited Liability Company 26, 73

Little Yellow Bird 52, 64

LLC/DE 51, 74, 75, 78

LLC/Partnership 51, 74, 75, 76, 78, 82, 85

M

Managers/Officers 28, 175

McDonald's Corporation 20, 65

McKinsey Global Institute 40, 65

Mission statement 17, 18, 19, 20, 48, 61

MSMEs 40

Multi-generational business 39,
70, 72, 86, 123, 170

N

Net Profit Margin 89, 90, 91, 93, 94, 95, 111

NPM 89, 91, 93, 96, 97, 98, 101, 111

O

One-purchased 18

Operating Profit Margin 91, 92, 115

OPM 92, 93, 115

Outland Denim 154, 177

P

Partnership 51, 64, 71, 74, 75, 76, 78, 79, 82, 85,
87, 132, 135, 136, 142, 143, 144, 145, 167, 168

Patagonia 149, 150, 151, 177

Performance ratios 95, 97, 98, 103

Plateau level compensation strategy 100, 101

Practice 37, 47, 110, 157, 179

Profit first businesses 23

Profits before people 23

Province Apothecary 78, 79, 126

Purpose statement 20, 21, 22, 27

R

Rand 159, 177

Reasonable Compensation 77, 97, 102

Reet Aus 119, 120, 126

Regenerative Organic Alliance 38, 65

Rule of 70 116

Rule of 72 116

S

Salt Spring Coffee 37, 38, 65

Scalability 51, 117, 118, 119

Scale 21, 40, 87, 115, 117, 118, 119, 120, 156, 176, 179

S corporation 20, 51, 65, 71, 74, 75, 76, 77, 78, 81, 85, 102, 106

SEWF (Social Enterprise World Forum) 65

Shareholder Value 56, 72, 103, 105, 106, 112

Slacktivism 56

Small Business Administration (SBA) 40, 65

SMEs 40, 64, 65

Social Enterprise World Forum 53, 65

soleRebels 70, 126

Someone Somewhere 163, 177

SRI (Sustainable and Responsible Investing) 63

Stakeholder group 26, 130, 131, 133, 134, 135, 136, 141, 142, 143

Steward-Ownership 50, 51

Stewardship Plan 34, 36, 37, 47, 48, 49, 67, 129, 130, 132, 133, 134, 136, 137, 138, 140, 141, 145, 146, 156, 165, 166, 168, 170, 176

Stewardship Spotlight 13, 23, 31, 37, 45, 52, 57, 63, 70, 78, 82, 87, 94, 103, 108, 113, 119, 125, 138, 146, 154, 158, 163

Succession planning vii, 44, 50, 51, 121, 124, 126, 132, 136, 143, 171, 174, 179, 180

Successor team 106, 112, 116, 121, 122, 123, 124

T

Tax conduit 71, 97

Tax-neutral exchange 76, 78, 85, 102

The Coca-Cola Company 65

The extra 23, 30, 42, 43, 48, 61, 67

The Happy Pear 94, 126

Three-Basket Cash Flow System 89, 91, 93, 97, 103, 111

Tier One 27, 28, 29, 31, 35, 39, 43, 44, 46, 49, 52, 56, 61, 68, 71, 78, 85, 90, 97, 110

Tier Two 27, 28, 36, 46

Tony's Chocolonely 31, 32, 65

Too Good To Go 103, 104, 126

U

United Nations 40, 65

U.S. Bureau of Labor Statistics 65

V

VAUDE 108, 126

Vision statement 21, 36

Voting Stock 81, 85, 150

W

Who Gives A Crap 113, 114, 126

World Bank Group 65

www.DavidGrauSr.com iv, 155

Y

Yvon Chouinard 149

NOTES

NOTES

NOTES

NOTES

www.ingramcontent.com/pod-product-compliance
Lightning Source LLC
Chambersburg PA
CBHW051754200326
41597CB00025B/4547